T0184699

Mobile Device Management

Markus Pierer

Mobile Device Management

Mobility Evaluation in Small
and Medium-Sized Enterprises

 Springer Vieweg

Markus Pierer
Vienna, Austria

ISBN 978-3-658-15045-7   ISBN 978-3-658-15046-4 (eBook)
DOI 10.1007/978-3-658-15046-4

Library of Congress Control Number: 2016947776

Springer Vieweg
© Springer Fachmedien Wiesbaden 2016

Printed on acid-free paper

This Springer Vieweg imprint is published by Springer Nature
The registered company is Springer Fachmedien Wiesbaden GmbH

Danksagung

An dieser Stelle möchte ich mich bei all jenen bedanken, die zur Entstehung des vorliegenden Fachbuches beigetragen haben und die mich in dieser Zeit physisch und psychisch unterstützt haben:

Meinen Eltern, die mir den Weg für das Studium geebnet haben und mich in all meinen Entscheidungen unterstützt haben. Meinen Schwestern, die in schweren Zeiten immer ein offenes Ohr für mich hatten, und meinen Freunden, die mich auch in schlecht gelaunten Phasen unterstützten.

Meiner Schwester, Univ. Doz. Monika Posadas Saucedo, für die kritische, konstruktive und präzise Durchsicht dieser Arbeit.

Den größten Dank möchte ich allerdings meinem kleinen Sohn, Jan-Markus aussprechen. Ohne seine Unterstützung wäre ein erfolgreicher Abschluss dieser Arbeit nicht möglich gewesen. Seine Geduld und Verständnis weiß ich sehr zu schätzen.

Vorwort

Enterprise Mobility Management spielt eine immer wichtigere Rolle in Unternehmen. Vor allem wenn es um Überwachung, Koordination, Optimierung und Unterstützung von Geschäftsprozessen geht. Aufgrund des raschen Wachstums der Mobilität in den letzten Jahren sind Unternehmen gezwungen, sich der Herausforderung der Integration mobiler Endgeräte – in die bestehende Infrastruktur – zu stellen. Durch die Einkehr von mobilen Endgeräten in das Betriebsumfeld ergeben sich neben einer Produktivitätssteigerung und Optimierung der Geschäftsprozesse allerdings auch viele Gefahren. Zudem sind, speziell in kleinen und mittleren Unternehmen in Österreich, das Bedürfnis und die Notwendigkeit für Enterprise Mobility Management-Systeme auf einzelne Geschäftsfälle reduziert. Ziel dieser Arbeit ist es, einen Einblick in Enterprise Mobility Management zu gewähren und herauszufinden, ob es für diverse spezielle Anforderungen einen allgemein gültigen Systemvergleichsansatz gibt, um Unternehmen die Auswahl des richtigen Systems zu erleichtern. Dazu werden wichtige Grundlagen des Enterprise Mobility Managements erläutert, mobile Endgeräte klassifiziert und Begriffsabgrenzungen vollzogen. Um verschiedene Systeme vergleichbar zu machen werden Funktionsbeschreibungen in Kategorien unterteilt und mittels Systemtests auf eine einheitliche, vergleichbare Basis gebracht. Bezugnehmend auf Fachliteraturen, Online-Beiträgen, Experteninterviews, Systemtests und Erfahrungen werden Problemfelder und Vorteile einer Enterprise Mobility Management-Systemeinführung dargestellt. Aus den daraus resultierenden Erkenntnissen werden spezielle Anforderungen im KMU Markt abgeleitet und mittels einer Umfrageauswertung, für einen Systemvergleich, gewichtet. Der Systemvergleich dient als Anhaltspunkt für Unternehmen – die bestrebt sind mobile Endgeräte in die bestehende Infrastruktur zu integrieren – um eine Systemauswahl durchführen zu können. Das Ergebnis dieser Arbeit zeigt auf, dass im KMU Markt spezielle Anforderungen gegeben sind, die bei einer Systemeinführung berücksichtigt werden müssen, es jedoch keinen fundierten Fahrplan für eine Systemauswahl gibt.

Foreword

The importance of enterprise mobility management is increasing in organizations. Particularly in cases of monitoring, coordinating, optimizing and supporting of business processes. Due to the rapidly growing market of mobility in the last few years, organizations are forced to face the challenges of integration of mobile devices in their existing information and communication infrastructures. The entrance of mobile devices in business environments enhances productivity and business process optimizations. However, this situation raises a lot of possible vulnerabilities and security leaks. Additionally, the awareness and the necessity is restricted to special business cases that enforce an application of enterprise mobility management systems. Especially, in the small and medium sized enterprise market in Austria. The purpose of this thesis is to gain an insight in enterprise mobility management and to find out, if there is a generic valid system comparison approach for various special circumstances in order to facilitate the selection process for organizations. Therefore important basics of enterprise mobility management are illustrated, mobile devices are classified and conceptual definitions are accomplished. To make various different systems comparable, feature descriptions are categorized. Through system tests, these features are brought to a common and comparable base. Referring to professional literature, online-articles, expert-interviews, system tests and experiences in the field of enterprise mobility, problem areas and benefits of an enterprise mobility management system introduction are pointed out. Based on upcoming findings, special circumstances in the small and medium sized market are derived. These requirements are weighted based on the results of a conducted survey. The system comparison serves as an indicator for organizations, which aims to integrate mobile devices in their existing infrastructure. Hence, it can be used to perform an enterprise mobility system selection. The result of this thesis shows that the small and medium sized enterprise market has special circumstances that have to be considered during an enterprise mobility management system introduction, however there is no concrete procedure for the system selection.

Table of contents

15

List of figures

List of tables

List of abbreviations

API	Application Programming Interface
App	Application
BYOD	Bring Your Own Device
CEO	Chief Executive Officer
COBO	Corporate Owned Business Only
COPE	Corporate Owned Personal Enabled
CTO	Chief Technical Officer
e.g.	for example (exempli gratia)
EMM	Enterprise Mobility Management
GPS	Global Positioning System
GSM	Global System for Mobile Communication
HTC	High Tech Computer Corporation
HTML	HyperText Markup Language
IDE	Integrated Development Environment
IMAP	Internet Message Access Protocol
IMEI	International Mobile Equipment Identity
IMSI	International Mobile Subscriber Identity
Inc.	Incorporation
IT	Information Technology
kg	kilogram
LAN	Local Area Network
LED	Light-emitting diode
LTE	Long Term Evolution

MAM	Mobile Application Management
MCM	Mobile Content Management
MDM	Mobile Device Management
MSM	Mobile Security Management
n.a.	Not available
NFC	Near Field Communication
OTA	Over The Air
PC	Personal computer
PIM	Personal Information Management
POP	Post Office Protocol
SMS	Short Message Service
UMTS	Universal Mobile Telecommunications Standard
VPN	Virtual Private Network
WebApp	Web application
WLAN	Wireless Local Area Network
WWW	World Wide Web

1 Introduction

Since the second generation of enterprise mobility and the consumeration of IT mobile devices are used everywhere. Not only privately, even in the business area they are omnipresent. The challenges regarding data protection, security and mobile device management are manifold. On that point of view the question, how to secure and manage a mobile device infrastructure, arises. Mobile device management systems take care about such challenges. It secures sensitive data, provides applications, changes and optimizes business processes and brings transparency in shadow IT. However, the market consists of more than one hundred different software vendors with varying supported feature sets. The wish of flexible, scalable, adaptable and comparable solutions is getting louder due to the fact that the right choice of a MDM system is still in the responsibility of organizations.

1.1 Problem area

Are there any trends that appear for an introduction of mobile device management? What are the main areas of interest and which solutions fit to special requirements? These are central questions regarding the thesis. Due to rapidly changing business requirements in organizations environment and a shortened life cycle in the information and communication field, flexible and scalable mobile device management solutions get more and more importance. To achieve the desired security level, companies search for new opportunities to maintain that issues. Especially, the small and medium sized market has special requirements which has to be addressed accordingly. That's the reason why MDM vendors focus on a broad range of functionality, which results in very high fees for interested parties. Additionally, the complexity increases and companies often struggle during the introduction. In order to survive in the daily business it is extremely important to adapt to the circumstances and respond as quickly as possible. This is one of the reasons why flexible, scalable and transparent solutions are necessary. The main task of the thesis is to evaluate the market regarding mobile device management. Finding demanded requirements, compare different MDM vendors and consider possible approaches regarding data privacy, data protection and types of mobile device management systems. The small and medium sized market is a segment which seeks for MDM solutions that are easily comparable. Moreover finding the right choice based on different requirements under the consideration of regulations and special circumstances is crucial.

1.2 Task description

The objective of the thesis is to illustrate why mobile device management is highly important in companies environment, to secure network, data and achieve the required confidentiality. Additionally, organizations are faced with countless different solutions and struggle to evaluate the best fitting for organizations environment. The reader should get a general understanding of mobile device management, its concepts and why it is highly important. Moreover the thesis focuses on special requirements in small and medium sized enterprises regarding mobile device management which are key points of a successful evaluation and introduction of an MDM product. Based on market researches, the evaluation and the needed requirements, a MDM solution is selected. Not part of the thesis are topics like the maintenance of mobile device management solutions, the development of extensions, phases during the introduction project and descriptions of API`s or the applicability for all mobile platforms. The audience, which are mainly Security Managers and safety-conscious managing directors, should get an awareness of MDM, its concepts, how to secure companies environment and what are important factors for a successful introduction of a MDM solution. Thereby for the general understanding no specific prior knowledge is necessary. Thus, this thesis serves for interested parties who wish to introduce MDM or search for a security solution for mobile devices.

1.3   Research questions / hypotheses

1. How does the market evolution effect companies environment?
    a. Which security policies are supported by mobile device platforms?
    b. Which functions enhance or restrict data privacy on different mobile device platforms?

2. How can the introduction of MDM systems be justified?
    a. What are the key drivers for the introduction of MDM systems?
    b. Which problems and benefits emerge while selecting a MDM product?

3. On which basis can MDM tools be evaluated?
    a. What are the prerequisites for the comparison of MDM solutions?
    b. Which are the most common requirements that emerge in organizations environment?
    c. What are the most important MDM criteria that are pursued in organizations environment while selecting a MDM solution?

1.4   Methods and expected results

For establishing the thesis, the methods of relevant literature, scientific works and publications are used. Those methods emphasize security concepts on different device types, general approaches of platforms and enterprise mobility strategies over the years. To achieve a comparison of different mobile device management products it's crucial to compare functions regarding Mobile Asset Management (MAM), Mobile Security Management (MSM), Mobile Content Management (MCM) and Mobile Application Management (MAM). A self-established feature matrix serves as a standard guideline, which aims to make MDM systems comparable regarding their functionality. Additionally, data privacy and data protection are considered to achieve a valuable comparison.

To react on special circumstances, customer needs, challenges and opportunities in the small and medium sized enterprise, a conducted survey and expert interviews highlight most important requirements and form the basis of a weighted evaluation criteria catalogue. In that context the criteria catalogue will serve as an indicator for a solution selection for small and medium sized enterprises in the future. Especially due to the fact that possible challenges, opportunities and market shares are outlined.

1.5 Structure

In the first chapters necessary fundamental terms of mobile device management are annotated and the market evolution is drawn. Enterprise mobility is brought into context to mobile device management and special mobile device types – which were placed on the market during the second generation enterprise mobility – are explained in detail. In combination with mobile platforms like Android, mobile devices are key drivers for mobile device management systems, hence the introduced concepts. Chapter 6 concentrates on the different concepts and areas of interest, especially the features that any MDM system has to fulfil in order to be competitive. This sub-chapter is an important component to understand the challenges and opportunities that emerge during an introduction of a MDM system. Legal regulations, data protection, utilized technologies and the power of controlling and auditing are emphasized. The main focus will be the evaluation of MDM systems for the small and medium sized market. The findings of a conducted survey are weighted and compared to determine the best suitable MDM system for small and medium sized enterprises. During the thesis, experiences and expert know-how underpins statements and spans connections to all enterprises to evaluate MDM systems based on their supported feature set.

2 Mobile Device Management (MDM)

In the following section the reader gets an introduction in mobile device management and its context to enterprise mobility management to emphasize the differences, characteristics and similarities of those concepts.

"Mobile Device Management (MDM) software secures, monitors, manages and supports mobile devices deployed across an enterprise. Enterprise-grade MDM functionality typically includes over-the-air distribution of applications, data and configuration settings for all types of mobile devices, including mobile phones, smartphones, tablet computer, ruggedized mobile computers, mobile printers, mobile POS devices, etc. The intent of MDM is to optimize the functionality and security of a mobile communication network while minimizing cost and downtime. This applies to both company-owned and employee-owned devices across the enterprise." (Johnson, 2011, p. 3)

To reach an optimal level of control, companies are forced to introduce security solutions for mobile devices. However, in the past MDM only focuses on getting control over devices and secure the information technology infrastructure environment. In that context MDM enabled chief technical officers to implement an optimal level of security, although devices potentially where located everywhere around the world. Through the consumeration of IT – that have brought consumers the possibility to use their mobile device for business activities, such as checking e-mails or using company based content – the demand on more flexible, scalable and granular systems have been growing enormously. That was the reason why enterprise mobility management (EMM) came into place.

"An enterprise mobility management (EMM) solution goes beyond managing mobile devices themselves and also provides capabilities to manage their content, including apps and their associated data, documents and other files, as well as e-mail. IT gains more granular, flexible ways to secure and control user mobility while providing greater freedom and a more convenient, productive experience for users." (Citrix TechTarget, 2013)

Enterprise mobility management typically involves:
- Mobile Device Management (MDM)
- Mobile Application Management (MAM)
- Mobile Content Management (MCM)
- Mobile Security Management (MSM)

Whereas mobile device management focuses on security and control issues, enterprise mobility management addresses a broader range of functionality concerns. It encompasses mobile device management, but allows additional settings for application and information management. However, due to marketing aspects and the historical background, mainly all software vendors term their enterprise mobility (EMM) products mobile device management (MDM). On the one hand that could be a misleading interpretation, but on the other hand it is justified by the development progress from the past. Vendors implement EMM features in their existing MDM solutions to enhance the product functionality. (Alms, 2008; Johnson, 2011; Cirtrix TechTarget, 2013)

3 Market size and evolution of MDM

As mentioned in the section Mobile Device Management (MDM), the market has evolved into an enterprise mobility management suited market. The first generation of mobile devices were designed for a local device management, where a technical engineer allowed or restricted data access. The usage of mobile phones was limited to calling and messaging functionality. The second generation of enterprise mobility mobile devices have capabilities to support company's business processes with mobile solutions, like mobile applications, data visualization methods or enhanced communication channels. Therefore the EMM market is growing quickly and the vendor landscape has changed significantly. Forbes (2013) pointed out that the adoption of mobile devices is one of the most widely adopted technologies since the adoption of PC`s in the 1980`s. The rapid growth of mobile devices like smart-phones, tablet computer or netbooks is a key driver for gaining more productivity and efficiency for organizations. Employees use their private devices for fulfil business tasks. Retrieving data, utilizing enterprise applications or accessing information is common today. However, these technologies have changed company's environment sustainably. The consumeration of IT, which is a phenomenon where consumers use new innovations not only privately, but also introduce it in the business world, brought a lack of security and an increasing demand of new IT infrastructure components. That circumstances have required a shift in IT integration strategies. The main characteristics of second generation mobile devices are:

- They can be reached merely over mobile networks or wireless LAN
- The location is never fixed
- The availability is not given to 100%
- Huge data amounts cannot be transmitted reliable
- All actions have to be done over the air, due to distribution issues
- Monitoring, controlling and reporting needs constantly remote actions
- The heterogeneity is widespread and different operating systems and firmware versions are used in the IT infrastructure.

(Forbes Inc., 2013; Kesten & Klett, 2012; Harris, Ives & Junglas, 2012; Sammer, 2013)

Based upon the given characteristics and the evolution of mobile device management the market size can be drawn. Basso and Redmann (2012) pointed out that the MDM market is a very fast growing market. The aforementioned evolution underpins that statement. Additionally they estimated the actual market value in 2012 over $500 million with more than one hundred different software vendors. The forecast until 2019 for the MDM market value has been announced with $3.94 billion, says Markets and Markets (2014) in their market forecast and analysis report. Based on the gathered data, the extrapolation at a constant distribution results in a market value of $2 billion in 2015.

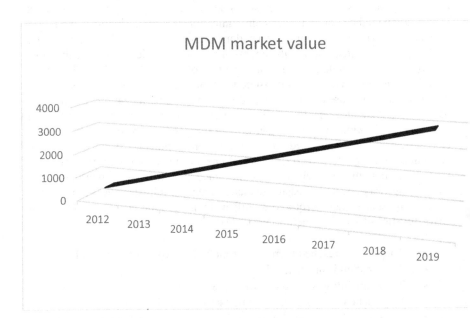

Figure 1: MDM market value

4 Mobile Device types

This section covers typical mobile devices that have second generation enterprise mobility capabilities and are used in company's environment. Due to data privacy and security policies companies seek for solutions to manage mobile devices accurately. In addition, operation and maintenance are crucial in consequence of the characteristics which were explained in chapter 3.

4.1 Notebooks

Figure 2: Samsung Notebook (Samsung Electronics, 2014)

General information
A notebook is a mobile device with similar capabilities like a personal computer. The processing unit, random access memory and the hard drive are powerful components. Moreover a notebook combines components like display, keyboard, speakers, touchpad and universal serial bus into one system. It is one logical unit that performs all tasks which are necessary for daily work activities. Together with appropriate software (e.g. Microsoft Office) it supports business activities.

Mobility information
The release of notebooks enabled mobility through the portability of their design (e.g. rechargeable battery). Nowadays, the notebook average weight is round about 2kg based on the size and equipment. Additionally, an USIM (Universal Subscriber Identity Module) allows access to organizations network environment or internet.

Operating system information
The operating system is identical to personal computers. The most adopted operating system all over the world is Microsoft Windows. The current version is 8.1. However, some other vendors like Apple and Linux possesses market share. (Kersten & Klett, 2012)

Conclusion
Companies generally applied security standards for stationary network environments. Based upon the specifications of personal computers and notebooks it is obvious that notebooks are managed and controlled in the same way. For example, the operating systems were designed for controlling over group policy in a windows server environment. However, mobile device management systems can integrate such devices accordingly (e.g. It is possible to allow or restrict access to mobile websites or webapps with MDM – systems).
(Samsung Electronics, 2014a; AirWatch Inc., 2014)

4.2 Tablet computer

Figure 3: Samsung Tablet

(Samsung Electronics, 2014)

General information
Tablet computers, also called tablets, are mobile devices which are categorized between notebooks and smart-phones. Tablets are equipped with common components like, processing unit, random access memory and hard drive as well as sensors. The additional equipment provides enhanced capabilities that support business processes. For example, a GPS sensor allows location based services to increase the productivity and efficiency of employees by planning routes. Additionally, tablets consist of a touch display that substitutes the keyboard and mouse.

Mobility information
Tablet computers can be seen as the portable brother of notebooks. A long battery life, together with a great usability design are key drivers for companies' to utilize it in a business environment. Wireless LAN and mobile broadband technologies support an exchange of information between employees and organizations.

Operating system information
The operation system depends on the hardware manufacturer. The most common used operating systems are:

- Apple iOS
- Google Android
- Microsoft Windows RT

Business applications need to be developed for specific operating systems and are available over the public app stores or via corporate app stores from organizations. (Kersten & Klett, 2012; TechTarget Inc., 2014)

Conclusion

Mobile Device Management (MDM) systems are conceived for such mobile devices. Security concerns, data protection and data privacy requires an adequate pillar, which is provided by MDM – systems. Hence, MDM vendors focus on such mobile devices with aforementioned operating systems. The enhanced functionality brings a lot of security risks with it, that have to be managed and controlled accordingly. Therefore, almost all MDM vendors have implemented mobile security measures in their products (e.g. secure file containers). (Samsung Electronis, 2014a)

4.3 Phablet

Figure 4: Samsung Phablet

(Samsung Electronics, 2014)

General information

Phablets are per design hybrid systems that have functionality of a tablet and a smart-phone at the same time. The equipment is typical for tablets which entail a processing unit, random access memory, hard drive, sensors and other common tablet components. As tablets and smart-phones, phablets enhance business process supporting activities. Moreover the USIM, together with call functionality provided by the operating system, allows conversations. The form factor, which is between four-and-a-half and seven inches, measured diagonally, allows an efficient, intuitive and fast work experience and therefore supports the productivity of employees as well as companies. In that context, phablets merge both functionalities – tablet and smart-phone – together in one mobile device.

Mobility information

As tablets are portable brothers of notebooks, phablets can be seen as smaller portable brothers with enhanced functionality. As aforementioned, the USIM allows conversations and the smaller form factor makes it easier to carry it around. Those aspects are key drivers for the utilization in business environments.

Operating system information

The operating systems for phablets are widespread like they are for smart-phones. Organizations can decide to go for either a closed platform like

- Apple iOS
- RIM – Blackberry

or an open platform like

- Google Android
- Microsoft Windows Phone
- Nokia Symbian

(Kersten & Klett, 2012; TechTarget Inc., 2015a)

Conclusion

Like tablets, phablets are mobile devices with a broad intended purpose. Mobile Device Management (MDM) systems focus on such devices. The operating systems and their system architectures form an enormous level of security concerns.

Closed platforms provide more security measures. Each developed app is proved by the operating system manufacturer before it is launched in the app store and the API`s (Application Programming Interfaces) are well defined. Besides closed platforms have limited and not expandable functionalities.

Open platforms provide more possibilities for third party vendors to introduce enhanced functionality and the API`s are more extensive. However, the flexibility causes security risks.

(Kersten & Klett, 2012; Sammer, 2013)

In consequence of data privacy and data protection issues, companies` have to integrate appropriate measures. Nevertheless, most companies have a hybrid system landscape which makes it more difficult to manage devices appropriately. Thus, MDM vendors support both platforms and provide necessary restrictions and policy guidelines.

4.4 Smartphone

Figure 5: Samsung smartphone
(Samsung Electronics, 2014)

General information
A smart-phone is a second generation enterprise mobility cellular telephone. Besides call functionality, it provides users with enhanced features like mobile browsing, texting, digital camera, personal information management or the ability to run apps. It is often used as a substitute for a notebook or personal computer, especially when mobility comes into place. With a high performing processing unit, a high amount of random access memory and sensors it allows for private and business actions. Checking e-mails, planning activities and appointments are some examples for business supporting activities of a smart-phone. The small form factor is, additionally, a key driver for increasing efficiency, mobility and productivity for employees and companies.

Mobility information
Smart-phones are portable devices with similar capabilities of phablets or tablets. However, they are smaller, handier and therefore used more often. The combination of mobility, portability, usability and the capabilities in the business field makes a smart-phone indispensable nowadays. Equipped with various communication interfaces (Wireless LAN, Bluetooth, NFC, LTE, ...) the smart-phone can exchange information and collaborate with traditional network infrastructures and landscapes.

Operating system information
As aforementioned in the section Phablet, smart-phones are based on either closed or open platforms. Even though, there is a huge amount of operating system vendors, the most common ones were enumerated previously and are discussed in chapter 5. (Kersten & Klett, 2012; TechTarget Inc., 2015b; Sammer, 2013)

Conclusion

Based upon the fact that the usage of smart-phones is overlapping in the fields of private actions and business activities, Mobile Device Management (MDM) systems are predestined to decouple those fields. Most systems respond to data protection and data privacy with the ability to separate apps, e-mails and other services into two profiles (work and personal).

A huge amount of different MDM – policies allow for restrictions in the usage of smart-phones for private actions. The chapter Categorization of MDM focuses more on details about special functionalities. (Samsung Electronis, 2014a)

4.5   Further mobile devices

Previous chapters focus on the most common mobile devices. Despite that, there are mobile devices that are still considerable. One of them is the *smartwatch*, which is a counterpart of a conventional clock. Besides time information, the smartwatch provides the user with additional information. Calling, texting and mailing are common, while using current smartwatches. However, most smartwatches are coupled to the smart-phone via Bluetooth to gather information. If manufacturers are going to introduce independent, Bluetooth decoupled smartwatches, and develop business applications for it, they probably will become third generation enterprise mobility devices that have to be monitored and controlled regarding data privacy and data protection. Baresch (2015) mentioned that, sensitive business data cannot stay on devices without any control mechanism thus they have to be managed accordingly. Moreover he pointed out that the same facts have to be considered with *glasses* – a wearable technology with an optical head-mounted display – and in the future with *cars*. The new generation of cars offer PIM (Personal Information Management) functionality out of the box. (Baresch, 2015; Sammer, et al., 2012; Open Automotive Alliance, 2015)

5 Mobile platform support

The chapter describes mobile platforms that are supported by different Mobile Device Management (MDM) system vendors. Although there are more mobile platforms available, which were mentioned in the previous chapters, below listed ones are most common, especially in enterprise mobility. Additionally, the small and medium sized market emphasizes the fact that notebooks are controlled in other environments as explained in the chapter Notebooks. Baresch (2015) stated out that some MDM vendors introduce controlling possibilities for notebooks and their operating systems, however the experience have shown that such capabilities are adopted poorly. Kantar Group (2014), which is one of the world's largest insight, information and consultancy networks, released an operating system market share report for November 2014 that shows the distribution of mobile operating system exactly. In Germany, more than 70% of smart-phone owners use Google Android followed by Apple iOS, Microsoft Windows Phone, RIM – Blackberry and others like Nokia Symbian.

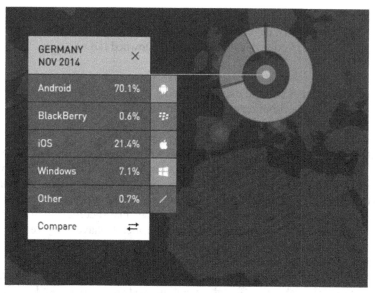

Figure 6: Operating system market share (Kantar Group, 2014)

Researching of different MDM solutions showed that functionalities of Mobile Device Management software products concentrate on those mobile operating systems and are highly important in the context of enterprise mobility.

5.1 Google Android

As mentioned in chapter 4, Android is an open platform which provides the possibility to introduce enhanced functionality. Mobile devices like smart-phones, tablets and phablets apply Android. Originally Android was developed by Android Incorporation. In 2005 Google bought Android Inc. and established the so called Open Handset Alliance, which is responsible for the further development of Android. Google's roles in the alliance are financing and marketing. Due to the open platform architecture many hardware manufactures offer Android for their mobile devices. Examples are Samsung, HTC, Sony and so on. The development of Android apps is based on well-established standards that includes Java and HTML. The focus on such standards allows the development of apps at low costs. Sammer, et al. (2014) declared two major advantages of Android regarding other operating systems:

- The easiness of development and deployment
- The cost-effective development with renowned IDEs

Those two advantages and the extensive model of privileges for mobile devices are key drivers for the adoption of Android around the world.

Regarding Mobile Device Management it has to be considered that interfaces to access device and operating system functionalities are different. Hardware manufactures and network providers adapt the operating system to gain a competitive advantage against their competitors. Those adaptations are called branding, which comprises enhanced functionalities like specific appointment or e-mail management. Although such features are nice to have, they restrict the Update and Patch management in MDM systems. In each update process, organizations have to choose the appropriate operating system based on the branding of the manufacturers and network providers. Moreover MDM vendors have to take care about different operating system versions and different brandings. That makes it difficult to introduce all MDM features in their products. Klünter (2014) a product manager of enterprise mobility stated, that the settings

38

for enterprise mobility are few. However, research has shown that most vendors introduce – based on market demands – such specific functionality settings. Michtell (2014) compared global players in mobile device management and found out that the newest version of operating systems and brands are supported by their MDM products. (Kersten & Klett, 2012; Sammer, et al., 2014; Klünter, 2014)

5.2 Apple iOS

Apple iOS and RIM-Blackberry are closed platform operating systems which provide a huge amount of security measures. The operating system is bound to Apple's hardware which consists of notebooks, tablets, smart-phones or media players. The common operating system makes it easier to collaborate under each other. The first version of iOS was launched in 2007 when the iPod came on the market. Together with appropriate Interfaces for third party software vendors Apple managed the balancing act between private and business adoption for the operating system. Native apps are developed with the X-Code IDE, which is the same as for desktop applications. Apple runs his own business. The IDE and the corresponding programming language (Objective C) are only compatible with Apple's mobile devices. Due to that facts the development of iOS apps is more expensive than Android apps. However, the closed platform architecture brings some important advantages with it:

- The closed File System
- Fast and reliable iOS Updates
- Enhanced security with sandboxing system
- Well-defined programming interfaces

Since iOS 4 Apple has released more than one-thousand-and-five-hundred new API's which provide extensive possibilities regarding mobile device management. Hence, companies always consider Apple hardware when they think of device management and business activities.

In an online article – mobile operating systems compared – Klünter (2014) explained that Apple's iOS is well established in the business world. Based upon the investigation of MDM vendors that statement can be approved. In an interview Bukowski (2015), Unit Manager at Seven Principles GmbH, validated Klünters statement. Additionally, he pointed out that – at a mobile device management point of view – it makes it much easier for MDM vendors, if hardware manufacturers and the network providers are not allowed to brand devices. A global trend of

segregating private from business information on all mobile devices was introduced by Apple with the release of iOS 7. Although the container principle is available for all other mobile operating systems, Apple was a pioneer in the development phase.
(Kersten & Klett, 2012; Sammer, et al., 2014; Klütner, 2014; Bukowski, 2015)

5.3 Microsoft Windows Phone

Despite the closed platform architecture of Apple's iOS, Microsoft Windows Phone is again an open platform operating system with all its limitations and advantages. In consequence of the huge market share of Microsoft's desktop operating system (Windows 8.1), the windows phone operating system has to be considered in all organizations around the world, when hardware and software selection comes into place. However, until 2010 Microsoft did not succeed in supporting multi-touch functionality for smart-phones or tablets in their mobile operating system. Due to that fact Android and iOS have gained a lot of market share in the mobile market. With the launch of Windows Phone 8.1, Microsoft released a product that has similar functionality as Android or iOS and is competitive. An increasing market share underpins it. Well known frameworks and integrated development environments form a solid pillar for the development of Windows Phone apps. The development is usually done with the programming languages C# and VB.NET. Sammer, et al. (2014) mentioned, in their book "Management von mobiler IT in Unternehmen", that Windows Phone is a very interesting platform for organizations. The compatibility between different devices is given through the similarity of an operating system product family. Other advantages of Windows Phone are:

- Native apps for Microsoft Office
- Universal app development for all Microsoft platforms
- Enhanced security with sand-boxing system

Klünter (2014) approved the advantages and mentioned that, since Windows Phone 8, Microsoft established a broad range of MDM API's. Additionally, they provide interfaces for third party vendors to introduce enhanced MDM functionality. Nevertheless, Microsoft is only at the beginning of the introduction of extensive MDM functionality. Very fundamental features regarding virtual private network, wireless network configuration, app pushing or container mode strengthen that opinion. But the awareness of Microsoft for mobile device operating system is - as aforementioned - high. Bukowski (2015) mentioned that,

40

since Windows Phone 8 has been launched, Seven Principle GmbH admitted all available features in their MDM software product and will enhance it regularly. In addition, the segregation of private and business activities – workspace container packages – will be provided for Windows Phone in the future. (Kersten & Klett, 2012; Sammer, et al., 2014; Klütner, 2014; Bukowski, 2015)

5.4   RIM Blackberry

Blackberry OS is a closed platform operating system, that runs only on Blackberry devices. In 1999 Research In Motion (RIM) released the first version of its operating system, which focused on supporting business activities. Personal Information Management (PIM) is one of the highlights of blackberry OS. It consists of functionality for texting, reading, checking e-mails, appointment management and other business activities. All of this features are based on highly secured information channels, which are encrypted accordingly. But since 1999, RIM has lost a lot of market share and is nowadays adopted rarely. Some strategic decisions didn't bring the desired results. The users were dissatisfied with mobile devices due to hardware and software restrictions. Therefore the market share decreased and Android, iOS and Windows Phone overtook Blackberry OS. Blackberry OS is written in C++, however apps are developed based on well-established standards that includes Java, HTML, C, C++ and Adobe Air. The concept is similar to Android, which results in low development costs. The major advantages of Blackberry OS was outlined by Sammer, et al. (2014) in their book "Management von mobiler IT in Unternehmen":

* Broad market for developers due to technology support
* The cost-effective development with renowned IDEs
* The strict separation of private and business data

Kersten & Klett (2012) underpinned those statements. Additionally they mentioned, that Blackberry OS has much more functionality than used. One example is the extensive over the air management, which forms a standard for other operating system vendors. With the newest release, Blackberry OS allows more than 450 different mobile device management settings. However, Klünter (2014) stated, that most companies should consider a Blackberry migration based upon the insecure future of RIM. Bukowski (2015) and Baresch (2015) share this statement. They further mentioned, that supporting a platform with low market share and an insecure future is not cost effective. (Kersten & Klett, 2012; Sammer, et al., 2014; Baresch, 2015; Bukowski, 2015)

41

5.5 Nokia Symbian

Symbian is an open platform operating system, that was mainly applied by Nokia smart-phones. In 2011 Nokia decided to apply windows phone in their smart-phones and has outsourced the further development of Symbian to Accenture. Symbian was one of the most popular mobile operating system in former days and therefore very widespread. Nokia supported business activities with a huge amount of business applications for Symbian. That was one reason why Symbian was used by organizations. However, since the emerging of Apple iOS, Android and Windows Phone, Symbian is applied rarely. Since the takeover of Nokia from Microsoft in 2014, Symbian lost market share again due to the fact, that Microsoft focuses on its own mobile operating system, Microsoft Windows Phone. Symbian itself supports a variety of application programming languages for their mobile applications. Developers can use C++, Java, Phyton, Ruby and more which makes mobile application development very interesting for a broad range of developers. The concept is again very similar to Android. Until 2010 Nokia released Symbian as an open source licence, which makes it interesting for the Symbian community to develop applications. Nokia profited from the business model because a lot of applications were released and more and more companies adopted Symbian. Sammer, et al. (2014) highlighted the advantages of Symbian in their book "Management von mobiler IT in Unternehmen" as follows:

- The cost-effective development
- Open source licence model
- A huge community

However the outsourcing of the further development with a change in the business model – licence fee model – and the takeover from Microsoft – as aforementioned – eliminated those advantages. Regarding Bukowski (2015) and Baresch (2015) Symbian is supported by most MDM vendors currently. Nevertheless MDM vendors will focus on market leaders because of the higher revenue ranges. Hence, Symbian will not be supported anymore in the future due to the ineffective business model. (Sammer, et al., 2014; Baresch, 2015; Bukowski, 2015)

6   Categorization of MDM features

This chapter gives an overview of the most important concepts, management perspectives, security concerns and main functions that have to be considered in order to introduce a mobile device management product and to go for a well-defined mobility strategy in organizations. Some concepts refer to problem areas and benefits of mobile device management which are discussed in the following chapters.

6.1   MDM categorization approach

The MDM categorization approach is the first step to establish a standard guideline feature matrix, which aims to make MDM systems comparable regarding their functionality. Prototype testing emphasizes features and integrates them into categories. Due to the manifold feature description of each system a categorization is necessary for an in-depth analysis. This chapter focuses on the categorization and brings various different features to a common denominator. The result of the chapter is a categorization, which serves to establish a feature matrix in chapter 0. Figure 7 illustrates an **overview of enterprise mobility management systems**, which are determined as categories for the feature matrix.

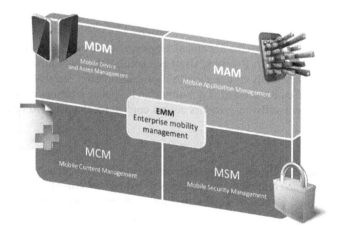

Figure 7: EMM overview

6.2 Mobile Asset Management

Mobile Asset Management describes a management approach for controlling, monitoring and optimizing mobile devices. The intent of mobile asset management is to get an accurate amount of data to control and monitor mobile devices in companies environment and to establish a database for registered mobile devices and their users. A comparison to local device management, which typically supports technical engineers to control and monitor stationary IT infrastructures shows the similarities and differences between the two approaches. However, in terms of mobile device management (MDM) and under consideration of local device management, asset management comprises following aspects and functionalities:

Mobile operating system support
Mobile device management solutions typically consist of a client/server architecture. A mobile client is installed on mobile devices to communicate with the server and exchange relevant data. It indicates the supported operating systems for mobile device management. That aspect was discussed in chapter 5.

IMEI/IMSI status
The international mobile equipment identity is a serial number. It is unique for every device and helps to identify the mobile device clearly. In mobile device management it is associated with an user and helps to determine which device is used by which user.

Roaming status
The roaming status helps the technical engineer to determine, which mobile network is used currently. Roaming itself is a technology that allows the user to set or receive phone calls or use mobile data transmission, no matter in which mobile network they are located. To monitor and regulate roaming costs, mobile device management software vendors set up control mechanisms to control the roaming status.

Battery status
The battery status delivers information about the battery consumption or the charge level for each mobile device. It helps to indicate whether the battery could be damaged or not. Hence, it is often used for inventory management.

GPS localization
The global positioning system (GPS) is a widely used functionality to locate mobile devices. It is often used to find stolen or lost mobile devices. It allows an exact localization of users or mobile devices and could therefore be used in many scenarios (e.g. route tracking for logistics).

Firmware information
The firmware usually gives information about the operating system. Usually the operating system version number is one of the most important ones. It helps technical engineers to analyse issues and concerns in order to ensure a smooth operation of mobile devices. Additionally, the firmware information is a pillar for the application management to figure out which application could be operated on mobile devices.

Mobile device manufacturer/model
Information about the mobile device manufacturer and the mobile device model are important informations, when special circumstances like container management comes into place. For example, some manufacturers or mobile device models don`t support container apps like Samsung KNOX. If an organization wants to go for a container solution to segregate private from business data, those information's are crucial.

Current language
Regarding application and security management, the current language could be highly important for technical engineers. In multinational concerns the language influences different security and applications settings.

Installed software and applications
Detailed statistics about mobile applications helps to determine possible security risks. If an organization wants to apply defined security standards, they have to consider mobile applications. Applications Black/White listings in mobile application management are further steps to secure mobile networks.

Service history
Shows the activities of the mobile device and the mobile user. Which activities were done when and by whom are central aspects of that feature. One typical scenario for service history logging could be the enrolment process of a mobile device. It defines the date, when the mobile device management system starts controlling the mobile device.

Network information
Network information shows connections to mobile networks, information exchanges via virtual private networks or mobile data usage. Such information supports the technical engineer by analysing possible security or network lacks.

Enrolment date
As described in the service history aspect the enrolment date indicates the date when a mobile device starts being controlled by a mobile device management system.

Last MDM-Client connection/inventory update
Because of the client/server architecture the client always has to communicate with the server to exchange data. In some cases the connection couldn't be established as defined it the mobile device management system. If an error occurs or if the inventory has to be updated a log entry is generated, which helps analysing changes in the environment.

Those features store and monitor relevant information of mobile devices. In the world of enterprise mobility management all of the mentioned features are part of the mobile device management (MDM). The core purposes of asset management are:

- Device registration
- Monitor, control and maintain mobile devices
- Decommissioning

Additionally, the EMM approach consists of mobile application management (MAM), mobile content management (MCM) and mobile security management (MSM) as described in chapter 2.

(Samsung Electronics, 2014; MobileIron Inc., 2015; 7P AG, 2015; Klünter, 2014)

6.3 Mobile Application Management

Mobile application management (MAM) is a term, that focuses on provisioning, controlling and maintaining mobile applications on mobile devices. The main purpose of MAM is to provide public and internally developed applications to end users automatically. Moreover, the provisioning of predefined applications and control of the usage can be achieved. In that context it is possible to establish a corporate app store with appropriate applications for mobile users, that can be distributed, controlled and maintained. Mobile application management and mobile asset management complement each other. Whereas mobile asset management ensures a high amount of control over mobile devices and the underlying hardware, mobile application management provides a high degree of control over mobile applications, from simple app wrapping to secure container applications. Mobile application management includes following aspects and functionalities:

Application installation and background installation
The ability of installing mobile applications over a mobile device management system is very helpful. Technical engineers have the possibility to define policies for application installation during the enrolment process of a mobile device. Based upon the strategy of organizations such an installation could be done in the background. Therefore it is possible to install necessary applications automatically when a new mobile device is introduced in the enterprise mobility management system.

Corporate App Store
The corporate app store is a store where business applications of organizations are provided to the mobile user. That could either be public applications from the public app stores like Google Play store or internally developed applications. In that context organizations have the possibility to provide a selection of allowed or tested applications and restrict the usage of all others. Additionally, the public app store can be deactivated.

Application blacklist/whitelist
Applications that are proved and tested are marked in whitelists whereas dangerous and insecure applications are marked in blacklists. Together with defined policies a technical engineer can monitor and control the application usage of mobile users. An application breach can notify the technical engineer and the appropriate measure can be executed (deinstalling of applications, encryption of sensitive data or data wipe).

Vendor App store deactivation
Although the black- and whitelists form a certain amount of application security, mobile users can download and install all applications from the public app stores. The deactivation of public app stores can impede the installation of prohibited applications. Despite the deactivation, sophisticated mobile users can install mobile applications directly without the public app stores. Therefore, policies like blacklist reporting are necessary. The main objective is to provide required apps in the corporate app store.

Mandatory applications
An organization can define some mobile applications as mandatory and install them during the enrolment process. The deinstalling of mandatory applications is reported to the technical engineer who reacts accordingly (e.g. re-installation of mobile application).

Active Sync/Corporate Exchange settings
When organizations operate a Microsoft exchange server, they tend to roll out the appropriate configuration directly on mobile device users. The parametrized settings can be rolled out to all users automatically, to connect them to their mailboxes.

E-Mail management
E-Mail management is the pendant to corporate exchange configuration and helps organizations that don't operate a Microsoft exchange mail server. The needed settings for IMAP or POP are rolled out automatically to the end users.

Per App VPN
Most organizations grant access to internal information technology structures for mobile users and their mobile devices. With per app VPN it is possible to grant mobile applications access to well-defined internal resources via a virtual private network. Each application connects itself to the internal infrastructure and receives and sends data over an encrypted tunnel.

Cost control management
Especially for call or data roaming it is highly important to control the costs and define limits when a data connection or phone calls are capped. Technical engineers can define limits of data volume or roaming costs to cap the connections if a mobile users is far beyond those limits.

Containerization/Sandboxing
Containerization or sandboxing is a concept, where organizations can enforce the usage of special container application that segregates the private from the business area. Samsung KNOX is such a container solution, which is described in the chapter 6.5. Secure File Container or Fizmo Safezone are two more, that enable the aforementioned segregation.

App Wrapping
Mobile applications can be wrapped to control and monitor the usage of mobile applications. App Wrapping is an interesting feature that allows organizations the control over public applications, that are needed for supporting business processes in an organization. Additionally, containerization using app wrapping is possible.

Block copy/paste
Some mobile applications allow copying and pasting files, folders or text between different mobile applications. To avoid copying sensitive data from the business area to the private area it is necessary to block such patterns. However, based on which mobile operating system is used, the possibilities of blocking patterns are limited (e.g. Android stores contacts on both areas).

App usage monitoring
For monitoring and optimizing mobile applications, it is convenient to gather informations regarding usage, performance or availability. With app usage monitoring an organization can react on mobile application lacks accordingly.

Remote desktop access
Nowadays mobile devices are used like personal computer for about twenty years. Business relevant activities are done with mobile devices and therefore remote support is necessary. The change of configuration or mail settings should work remotely, due to the fact that mobile users a rarely in house for getting support.

The aforementioned features make it possible to control and monitor the usage of mobile applications and define an appropriate level of security on the application layer. To secure sensitive data, is either a demand of organizations to avoid a loss of competitive advantages and furthermore regulated by law.

(Bundeskanzleramit RIS, 2015; BSI, 2013; 7P AG, 2015; Kersten & Klett, 2012)

6.4 Mobile Content Management

Mobile content management (MCM) is a set of technologies that focuses on the provisioning, controlling and monitoring for the secure access on corporate data and data transmission on mobile devices like smart-phones, tablets and other mobile endpoints. The main purpose of mobile content management is to provide and share files among different network connections. That could either be file shares on the local area network of an organization or data repositories for mobile clients. Moreover, mobile content management should define a set of policies for the access of data and control and monitor unauthorized access. Whereas mobile asset management and mobile application management focuses on securing mobile devices and applications, mobile content management ensures the secure file exchange between mobile endpoints. In that context mobile content management provides mobile applications with necessary data to incorporate with the local information technology infrastructure. The main areas of interest in mobile content management are:

Data management
To ensure efficiency and productivity, organizations have to provide necessary content on to go for the mobile users. To create, change, delete and annotate files and folders is crucial to support business processes. For example, sales representatives need current sales material in order to provide customers with accurate offers. Additionally enterprise resource planning can be supported by creating orders and invoices directly on the fly.

PIM (Personal Information Management)
Personal information management is a fundamental part of each mobile user. Store contact information of customers, administrate calendar and appointments or checking e-mails are personal information that allow each employee to fulfil his business tasks.

Document management software support
Support for document management software becomes highly important if organizations have introduced collaboration software like Microsoft Sharepoint. Special application programming interfaces have to be considered in mobile applications that allow the access to document libraries and other relevant data.

Data Synchronisation
The automatic synchronization of data is very important as mentioned in the data management feature above. Supporting flexible business workflows to achieve profitable interactions with internal and external stakeholders is crucial for every organization nowadays.

Data push
Data push is a mechanism, where important documents and files are pushed directly to a mobile device or a folder of a mobile device. In the context of up-to-date information, data push becomes important to increase the productivity of mobile users. Mobile device management systems allow a fast accurate way to provide necessary information as fast as possible.

Secure web browsing
Since the upcoming of the internet, web browsing and gathering accurate information in the World Wide Web is important for any organization. However, searching for web content could cause harm and increase security vulnerabilities. Despite those facts, organizations provide business relevant content to mobile users. Such content and especially the connection to internal resources need to be secured (e.g. encrypted).

Encrypted mail attachment
Mail attachment encryption is applied in order to prevent any unexpected intermediary access to e-mail content. Referring to mobile container applications, it is very important to guarantee the strict segregation of private and business area. Moreover it avoids, that sensitive data could be read by not related persons.

Mobile content management (MCM) cooperate itself with mobile application management (MAM). On the application layer, mobile application management provides the needed control over mobile applications, which are needed to consume, edit or delete content. Mobile content management serves as middleware to provide content and information to the application layer on a highly secure level. These two approaches ensure compliance with regulatory regarding data privacy law.

(Bundeskanzleramt RIS, 2015; 7P AG, 2015; MobileIron Inc., 2015; AirWatch Inc., 2014)

6.5 Mobile Security Management

Mobile Security Management is a management approach for protecting and verifying mobile users. It is responsible for the enforcement of policies to registered mobile devices. The purpose of security management is to restrict or allow a defined level of settings troughout the whole environment. Moreover the configuration and implementation of control measures, the verification of the integrity and the detection of threats and weaknesses are intents of mobile security management. The primary functions and features of mobile security management are outlined below.

KIOSK Mode
The KIOSK mode is a special mode with defined restrictions and functionalities. Users are not allowed to leave the mode and use their smart-phone for other purposes than they were originally intended. The KIOSK mode is often used in scenarios like airplanes where passengers use the entertainment system but no other functionalities of the operating system.

Samsung KNOX
With a KNOX policy an organization can enforce the usage of the Samsung KNOX container. That feature is only available for KNOX capable devices, which are mainly Samsung devices. However, the KNOX mode guarantees a very high level of security in hardware, software and directly on the application level. Additionally, the container mode segregates private from business data. On the business side sensitive data is automatically encrypted and only available there.

Passcode/Password
The policy defines the accurate level of passcode or password security. A certain number of alphanumeric letters, digits and special characters. Those policies could be enforced so that the mobile user has to enter a passcode or password any time after the device is waked up from the hibernate mode.

Mobile device reset
The mobile device reset feature allows a technical engineer with the privileges, to reset the mobile device of a user remotely. Such policies are interesting if a user loses the mobile device or if it is stolen. It ensures data privacy and data protection.

Maintain mobile device lock
To lock or unlock a mobile device remotely is a feature that is very important, if remote configuration or control comes into place. Technical engineers have to unlock the device in order to be able to change configuration settings. Additionally, to lock the mobile device could be helpful to enforce an immediate passcode/password policy.

Prohibit Application installation/uninstallation
In some cases, after the requirements definition, organizations decide to prohibit the usage of certain applications. On the other hand it`s possible to prohibit the deinstalling to enforce the usage. Depending on the mobile operating system the user can install or deinstall the application, which generates a log entry or a report for the technical engineer to react on such a behaviour.

Maintaining Certificates
Certificates are used to establish a secure connection. Such certificates can be used to identify users or other devices like a web server. The distribution of certificates brings a user the needed privileges (e.g. data exchange or application usage).

Mobile device encryption
The encryption is a security feature that secures data, folders, e-mails and the operating system itself against an unauthorized access. While the mobile device is encrypted it isn`t possible to get any information at all. Especially in health care, where sensitive data exists, device encryption is highly important.

Anti-virus support
Since the consumeration of IT and the second generation enterprise mobility anti-virus support have to be considered in all environments. Malware, Spyware or Trojan horses entered in the mobile operating systems market and they have the potential to cause a lot of damage. Therefore anti-virus applications on mobile devices have to be evaluated and introduced.

Device compromise detection (root/jailbreak)
Some sophisticated users try to compromise their mobile device. That means, that they try to root it to get more insights and privileges of the operating system. Others try to jailbreak their device, to be able to use any network provider they want. Such compromises must be observed and appropriate measures have to be defined (e.g. data wipe or device reset).

Mobile device actions
The equipment of mobile devices, forces mobile device management products to prohibit or allow a huge amount of settings regarding security. Organizations have to define policies and measures for the usage of camera, mobile hotspots, Bluetooth, wireless connections or container enforcement.

Data loss prevention
Data loss could cause monetary damages, as well as competitive advantages against competitors. Data loss prevention is therefore very important for most organizations around the world. That is again a reason, why organizations enforce the usage of container applications to avoid the unencrypted storage of sensitive data locally on the mobile device. Technical engineers could wipe mobile devices remotely, if such a data loss is detected by the mobile device management system.

Mobile VPN
Mobile virtual private networks allow the connection of mobile devices to a local information technology infrastructure. With a mobile virtual private network, mobile devices can exchange information, gather and maintain data within the organization directly with the mobile device. If connections to the organizations infrastructure are necessary a VPN profile has to be installed on the mobile device.

Single-Sign On support
Single sign on itself describes the authorization of a mobile user on many applications with only one credential. Especially when a lot of applications are used to support business processes in an organization, single sign on is a convenient way to authorize a mobile user.

When an organization plans to implement an enterprise mobility strategy, it has to consider mobile application management (MAM), mobile device management (MDM), mobile content management (MCM) and mobile security management (MSM). Those four areas has to be brought into context with each other to guarantee an accurate level of secure enterprise mobility. The mobile security management purpose can not only be seen as isolated. Within the approach and the aforementioned intents mobile security management defines mobile device policies and measures for all four areas and let the system react on changes. Bukowski (2015) stated that the main goal of security management is to set policies and restrictions to maintain, monitor, control and enforce a defined mobile device policy set.

(Samsung Electronics, 2014; Kersten & Klett, 2012; MobileIron Inc., 2015)

7 Identified problem areas in SME`s

The chapter deals with challenges and problem areas of mobile device management, that have to be taken into account during an introduction of MDM. Some of the below specified challenges emerge due to the used technologies on mobile devices. Others have to be considered to be compliant with regulatory. Especially, the small and medium sized enterprise has special circumstances regarding security, data protection, type of MDM system, roll-out and over the air data transmission that are considered in the MDM evaluation in chapter 0. During an introduction any organization has to make decisions on these topics that influence the introduction and selection approach. Based on market research and expert interviews the most common problem areas were identified and are explained in detail below. Additionally, the chapter highlights the demand of all areas of enterprise mobility management (MDM, MAM, MCM and MSM).

7.1 Types of MDM systems

The type of mobile device management server has to be defined at the beginning of each MDM project. MDM server are offered in two different variations:

- Hosted / cloud based
- On-premise / in-house

An organization has to take the first strategic decision on which direction is to be pursued.

On-premise solutions provide maximal flexibility, regarding local information technology infrastructure connection and patch management of the MDM server. Additionally organizations can control the whole environment itself. If the integration of existing systems is necessary an on-premise solution offers such possibilities. However, on-premise MDM servers are much more expensive than hosted MDM servers. Besides efforts for updating, an organization has to train employees for maintaining the MDM server, install additional third party applications for containerization, corporate app store or security patches. Due to the higher capital costs of additional hardware and software maintenance, organizations firstly try to establish a solution with cloud based MDM servers. Software as a service (SaaS) is a service, that is offered by most MDM vendors nowadays. The MDM server is hosted by the vendor in their system landscape and provide necessary applications out of the box to run the mobile device management system optimally. Especially for small and medium sized enterprises, such a scenario is more beneficial, because of aforementioned high entry and maintenance costs of an on-premise solution. In a cloud based solution the software vendor takes care about maintenance and updates. Nevertheless, the requirements engineering process is more complex if organizations want to use a hosted MDM server. It has to be evaluated, which requirements are covered by hosted MDM server solutions. Some solutions do not offer a total integration to existing systems, which could be a reason for exclusion. Moreover it has to be considered that all data, even business data and sensitive personal information, is stored on external servers. Business critical data is given outside to a partner. Therefore special service level agreements have to be signed to avoid the abuse of data usage. (BSI, 2013)

7.2   Operating system security

The consumeration of IT as explained in the chapter 2 brought a lack of security in the business world. Especially when private mobile devices are used for business purposes. The mobile operating systems like Android, iOS or Windows Phone were originally designed for private usage. Only Blackberry OS was designed exclusively for business purposes, which is one reason why it was adopted widely. Based upon those facts, organizations have to ask themselves, which operating system should be supported for daily business activities. The global players introduced a lot of security features in their operating system to provide an accurate amount of security to organizations. Sandboxing is such a feature. Mobile applications consume data and information and the operating system restricts the access to other applications. No file exchange between applications is allowed, which secures sensitive information against abuse. Containerization is another concept, that most operating system vendors introduced or support via third party vendors. Bukowski (2015) and Baresch (2015) stated out, that operating systems that do not support sandboxing or containerization shouldn't be used in business environments. In a business world, where mobile devices are used, very strict security policies and measures play a vital role. In that context it is a key fact, that organizations have to choose wisely, which operating system is adopted or allowed for business activities. The adoption of diverse operating systems brings a lot of security risks and it does not imply, that each configuration and security setting can be implemented in every mobile device management system equally. The architecture of the operating systems and the open or closed platform approach brings system specific differences with it. Whether it is the provisioning of mobile application or application programming interfaces. In order to secure mobile devices and the used information, only the operating system platform specific configuration settings like – encryption or passcode policy – can be used. BSI (2013) emphasizes in a mobile device management report, that a strict segregation between business and private usage is only possible if a mobile device management system is implemented. Additionally, container solutions have some restrictions. Stored personal information – contact details – have to be shared through the container to the native operating system so that the contact information can appear on the display. (BSI, 2013; Klünter, 2014; Basso & Redmann, 2012)

7.3 Data protection

Data protection is a sensitive topic all over the world. Especially in a mobile environment it is very important to secure data communication, mobile devices and the whole mobile device infrastructure. Referring to chapter 7.1, the selection of the right MDM system types has to be considered. There are a lot of MDM software vendors that offer a cloud based solution with servers anywhere in the world. However, data privacy law is regulated differently in every country. Organizations have to take care about data communication and stored information on servers outside their original founding country. Otherwise, compliance with the associated data protection law cannot be guaranteed. MDM vendors underlie data protection regulations in their country, but definitely not in countries of their customers. Due to the rapidly increasing software as a service business area, most countries have established arrangements under each other. However, such arrangements focus more on data transmission between different countries. Safe Harbor is such an arrangement between the European Union and the United States of America. The contract regulates data transmission but does not guarantee that European data protection is given. For Austrian organizations the *"Datenschutzgesetz (DSG)"* regulates date privacy and data protection. (BSI, 2013; Kersten & Klett, 2012)

The data protection law indicates the following regulations:

„(1) Für alle Organisationseinheiten eines Auftraggebers oder Dienstleisters, die Daten verwenden, sind Maßnahmen zur Gewährleistung der Datensicherheit zu treffen. Dabei ist je nach der Art der verwendeten Daten und nach Umfang und Zweck der Verwendung sowie unter Bedachtnahme auf den Stand der technischen Möglichkeiten und auf die wirtschaftliche Vertretbarkeit sicherzustellen, daß die Daten vor zufälliger oder unrechtmäßiger Zerstörung und vor Verlust geschützt sind, daß ihre

Verwendung ordnungsgemäß erfolgt und daß die Daten Unbefugten nicht zugänglich sind.

(2) Insbesondere ist, soweit dies im Hinblick auf Abs. 1 letzter Satz erforderlich ist,

1. *die Aufgabenverteilung bei der Datenverwendung zwischen den Organisationseinheiten und zwischen den Mitarbeitern ausdrücklich festzulegen,*

2. *die Verwendung von Daten an das Vorliegen gültiger Aufträge der anordnungsbefugten Organisationseinheiten und Mitarbeiter zu binden,*

3. *jeder Mitarbeiter über seine nach diesem Bundesgesetz und nach innerorganisatorischen Datenschutzvorschriften einschließlich der Datensicherheitsvorschriften bestehenden Pflichten zu belehren,*

4. *die Zutrittsberechtigung zu den Räumlichkeiten des Auftraggebers oder Dienstleisters zu regeln,*

5. *die Zugriffsberechtigung auf Daten und Programme und der Schutz der Datenträger vor der Einsicht und Verwendung durch Unbefugte zu regeln,*

6. *die Berechtigung zum Betrieb der Datenverarbeitungsgeräte festzulegen und jedes Gerät durch Vorkehrungen bei den eingesetzten Maschinen oder Programmen gegen die unbefugte Inbetriebnahme abzusichern,*

7. *Protokoll zu führen, damit tatsächlich durchgeführte Verwendungsvorgänge, wie insbesondere Änderungen, Abfragen und Übermittlungen, im Hinblick auf ihre Zulässigkeit im notwendigen Ausmaß nachvollzogen werden können,*

8. *eine Dokumentation über die nach Z 1 bis 7 getroffenen Maßnahmen zu führen, um die Kontrolle und Beweissicherung zu erleichtern."*
(Bundeskanzleramt RIS, 2015, pp. 14-15)

§14 and §15 of the data protection law regulates data processing of personal and sensitive data. Even if data is processed by different agencies like MDM vendors who store data on their server, the organization is still responsible for the compliance with the data protection law.

7.4 Roll-Out

After having defined organizations requirements, security policies, type of MDM system and having considered possible data protection issues, organizations have to think about a roll out strategy to enrol all mobile devices, which belong to them or have to be managed over a mobile device management system. This phase is one of the most critical ones, because it directly impacts the mobile end users, from part-time staff all the way up to the CEO. For any mobile device a profile has to be activated by the end user to enrol the mobile device in order to be automatically manageable by the mobile device management system. The enrolment process ensue over the air (OTA) in four different steps:

- Authentication of the mobile user to a web portal
- Installation of the mobile device management client
- Provisioning of mobile device management certificates
- Configuration of the mobile device

Another challenge of organizations is the heterogeneity of the mobile device landscape. If different operating systems are supported, organizations have to consider operating system security concerns. Additionally, the provisioning of paid mobile application is a challenging thing. Apple provides a volume purchase program to support the distribution of application to all mobile end users. Android doesn't support the automatic roll out of paid mobile applications. If Android have been chosen the mobile end user has to install such mobile application manually. Obviously the end user is heavily involved in those process steps. Without the cooperation of the mobile users, the enrolment and application distribution cannot take place and further control and maintenance is difficult.
(Kersten & Klett, 2012; BSI, 2013; Klünter, 2014)

7.5 Over the air (OTA)

Over the air denotes a standard for remote configuration settings, which is totally carried out without any physical connection between the mobile device and the mobile device management server. Any kind of data transmission happens over wireless networks. Wireless connections can be established via:

- NFC (Near Field communication)
- Wireless local area network (WLAN)
- Bluetooth
- Mobile communication standards (GSM, UMTS, LTE)

On the one hand controlling, monitoring and maintaining mobile devices over the air is very comfortable. On the other hand it is a security risk and has some restrictions. To enforce security policies (e.g. lock and wipe a mobile device) or gather inventory data is common and easily feasible. To backup or update mobile devices remotely isn`t possible at the time. Therefore the mobile end user has the responsibility to care about mobile device updates and backups. Different MDM vendors are in negotiations with mobile device manufactures to introduce an application programming interface for it. Additionally, data transmission over wireless networks can`t be controlled and therefore has to be encrypted or secured over a virtual private network.

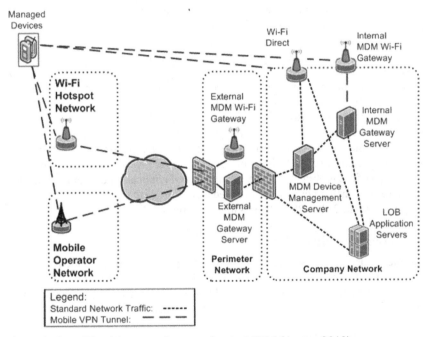

Figure 8: Over The Air secured connection to MDM (Asgar, 2013)

8 Justification of EMM utilization

The chapter focuses on possibilities and benefits of mobile device management, which justify an introduction of a mobile device management system. Some of the below explained benefits have been specified previously in the thesis and should now help to understand the demand of mobile device management systems. Others make it more convenient and more pleasant for organizations in their daily work and are key drivers for the introduction of a mobile device management system. Based on market research, expert interviews and professional experience in the field of mobile device management the most important identified benefits are explained in detail below. These benefits are considered in the MDM evaluation in chapter 0.

8.1 Homogeneous concept

A mobile device management system is a central element to establish and enforce security policies. From that point of view a MDM system follows a homogeneous concept and helps technical engineer to guarantee compliance with defined organization standards. Without security policies the effort of controlling, maintaining and monitoring a mobile device infrastructure is huge. The concept of MDM systems can be categorized in following areas:

- Definition of security policies
- Distribution of policies over the air
- Controlling, maintaining and monitoring the compliance
- React on policy breaches

The categorization is easy to maintain and can be applied in any mobile device management system. From the definition of policies to reporting security breaches the mobile business process can be controlled homogeneously. MDM systems accomplish a possibility to comply with legal rules, security demands and support the business strategy of an organization regarding productivity, security and efficiency. (Kersten & Klett, 2012; Basso & Redmann, 2012)

8.2 Monitoring and auditing

As mentioned in the chapter 8.1, controlling, maintaining and monitoring a mobile device infrastructure is only possible with a mobile device management system. Furthermore monitoring and auditing ensures legal compliance regarding data protection and data privacy. With mobile device management system configurations, mobile device system informations can be gathered, which deliver the status of each mobile device to the central controlling unit. Besides the connection, the storage and the application of data the mobile device management system can also enforce security policies and react on security breaches accordingly. To apply data protection regulations the following security policies have to be enforced and monitored constantly:

- Passcode or password policy
- Remote wipe policy
- Deactivation of wireless connections
- Containerization policy
- ...

The challenge of data protection focuses on compliance with regulations. To counteract such a challenge, monitoring and auditing was established. Information about data processing of personal and sensitive data is audited and logged to control and maintain a mobile device infrastructure environment. Additionally, monitoring and auditing helps to optimize security policies and guarantees, that legal compliance is given. In case of a loss of a mobile device with sensitive data stored on it, an organization has to be able to wipe data or lock the phone remotely. The data protection law (DSG 2000) points out, that organizations and the general manager privately are liable, if such security policies are not introduced. Bukowski (2015) underpins this statement in an expert interview.

(Bundeskanzleramt RIS, 2015; Bukowski, 2014; Kersten & Klett, 2012)

8.3 Incident and problem management

The chapter's Homogeneous concept, Monitoring and auditing, Operating system security and Data protection engage a lot with legal regulations. However, in a mobile business world, where mobile users are anywhere around the world, the demand of support in case of incidents and problems has to be considered. If a mobile device management system has not been introduced monitoring, auditing and especially, remote support cannot be given. Most incidents and problems occur after a firmware update or after a release of a new version of a mobile application. In a mobile business where mobile users are distributed around a wide region or world-wide, the management of incidents and problems is quite difficult. However, the mobile user requires support to ensure the correctness of his business activities and to be productive and efficient. Therefore mobile device management systems are necessary. Incident and problem management cooperates with monitoring and auditing to gather information. Log files, screen shots or system informations help technical engineers to provide accurate support for the mobile users. With third party vendors it is possible to provide remote support for the end users, which is a comfortable way the eliminate incidents or problems. (7P AG, 2015; Klünter, 2014; Kersten & Klett, 2012; Basso & Redmann, 2012)

8.4 Mobile device initiatives

Under the consideration of costs, productivity and efficiency most organizations have to decide which initiative they want to pursue. The three initiatives are:

- *BYOD* (Bring Your Own Device)
- *COPE* (Corporate Owned Personal Enabled)
- *COBO* (Corporate Owned Business Only)

BYOD is an initiative, that allows a mobile end user the usage of his private owned mobile device for business purposes. The advantages of BYOD are manifold. In the second generation enterprise mobility, end users tend to use their favourite mobile devices which helps to increase their user experience. The familiarity with the mobile device leads to more productivity and efficiency. The total investment for organizations decreases because of the fact, that the end user brings his personal owned mobile device into the organization. However, organizations have to consider that the heterogeneous infrastructure needs more attention and therefore maintenance costs will increase. In Chapter 7.2 the heterogeneous infrastructure risks were explained. Additionally, monitoring and auditing are much more complex. A data wipe will delete all data on the mobile device – even the private data of the mobile user. If an organization plans to implement a BYOD initiative, special agreements with the mobile user have to be signed (e.g. allow private data deletion).

COPE is an initiative where the organization buys the mobile device for the mobile end user. The mobile user is allowed to utilize the mobile device privately. The initial investment for the organization is high but auditing and monitoring is inexpensive. Moreover, the familiarity of the mobile device to the end user is given, because end users tend to utilize their favourite mobile devices for business purposes. Therefore productivity and efficiency increases. Mobile end users have to consider that a data wipe is allowed without any agreements. Backup and restore technologies are pursued by the mobile end user.

With *COBO* the organization buys the mobile device, but the usage is restricted to business purposes. The private usage of such a mobile device is strictly prohibited. Such an initiative is chosen, if sensitive information is stored extensively on the mobile device. Therefore special encryption mechanism and security policies are introduced. It is often used in the health care and investment sector.

In general, a combination of those initiatives is used in organizations. In departments, where sensitive data is stored extensively, it is advisable to choose the COBO initiative. If initial investment is important, the BYOD initiative is the best way. The COPE initiative is utilized rarely due to high investment costs and trends like selective data deletion.
(TechTarget Inc.. 2013; Kersten & Klett, 2012; BSI, 2013)

9 MDM evaluation for small and medium sized enterprises

This chapter focuses on the market evaluation for small and medium sized enterprises with special circumstances regarding feature support, legal compliance and technical support. At the beginning a market overview is given, which helps to preselect MDM vendors based on the market segmentation. Through market share, feature support and qualitative aspects like language support and licence fees, the MDM vendor list is shortened and analysed in detail.
A conducted survey emphasizes special organization requirements which are weighted to establish a suitable ratio between functionality and demand. Finally the various products are compared, to filter out the best suitable MDM system for small and medium sized enterprises in Austria.

9.1 Applied procedure for establishing a feature matrix

The categorization of MDM features – chapter 6 – delivers the input for the self-established feature matrix and an in-depth MDM system analysis. Prototype testing emphasizes functionality and operating system support of each MDM system under the consideration of identified problem areas and benefits. Each feature of the categories is rated based on the supported operating systems. The result of the feature matrix is used in the solution comparison in chapter 9.3.3 in order to find the best suitable MDM system for the SME market.

9.2 Market overview

As chapter 3 emphasizes, the mobile device management market is a very fast growing market with high competition. Business processes are supported by mobile devices like smart-phones or tablets. Aforementioned problem areas and benefits make it interesting to adopt mobile device management. Enterprise security, compliance with regulations, mobile optimization and possibilities to control, maintain and monitor mobile infrastructures are key drivers for the introduction in organizations. Due to the high amount of different mobile device management vendors and diverse feature descriptions, it is very difficult to select the right MDM vendor. The question which MDM system should be used, arises in every organization that plans to introduce such a system. Gartner Inc. (2013) released the magic quadrant for mobile device management software that is often used to make purchase decisions.

Figure 9: Magic Quadrant for Mobile Device Management Software
(Gartner Inc., 2013)

Although the magic quadrant indicates market leaders, visionaries, challengers and niche players and gives a certain overview, it does not consider special circumstances in the small and medium market. Due to researches and expert interviews following circumstances are relevant:

- Language support (mail and phone)
- Mobility managed services (outsourcing of operations)
- Regular consultation
- Direct support
- Licence fees

Based on that, the MDM vendor list had been reduced to five out of over hundred common solutions. At the beginning each vendor is introduced and business models, advantages and disadvantages of mobile device management systems are highlighted. In the end a detailed enterprise mobility evaluation examines obstacles and benefits of each MDM system.
(Bukowski, 2015; Baresch, 2015; Gartner Inc., 2013)

66

9.2.1 Citrix

Figure 10: Citrix Inc.
(Citrix Inc., 2015)

Citrix Systems Incorporation is a company located in the United States of America. The primary focus of Citrix is upon cloud based services in all fields of information technology. With the acquisition of Zenprise, which was one of the mobile device management software leaders, citrix entered into the market. The MDM product of Citrix is called XenMobile and has a broad set of functionality in all areas of mobility. The business model is strictly divided into two areas. MDM only, which offers a mobile asset management and a mobile security management. The second solution consists of a mobile application management and a mobile content management with special designed mobile applications, like Citrix WorkNotes to guarantee secure note taking. It is not possible to purchase functionalities on a modular base. Besides that, Citrix offers an on-premise and cloud based mobile device management system.

Advantages of Citrix XenMobile
- Market leader
- Technology specialist
- Broad range of MDM features
- Containerization for all device types

Disadvantages of Citrix XenMobile
- Tries to focus on cloud based services
- No focus on small and medium business

(Citrix Inc., 2015; Gartner Inc., 2013)

EMM capabilities

Feature	Android	iOS	Windows Phone 8	Blackberry OS	Symbian
Mobile Asset Management					
IMEI/IMSI status	✓	✓	✓	✓	✓
Roaming status					
Battery status	✓	✓	✓	✓	✓
GPS localization	✓	✓	✓	✓	✓
Firmware information	✓	✓	✓	✓	✓
Mobile device manufacturer	✓	✓	✓	✓	✓
Mobile device model	✓	✓	✓	✓	✓
Current language	✓	✓	✓	✓	✓
Installed software	✓	✓	✓	✓	✓
Service history	✓	✓	✓	✓	✓
Network information	✓	✓	✓	✓	✓
Enrolment date	✓	✓	✓	✓	✓
Last MDM-client connection	✓	✓	✓	✓	✓
Last inventory update	✓	✓	✓	✓	✓
Certificate validity	✓	✓	✓	✓	✓
Activation lock status	✓	✓	✓	✓	✓
Supervised status		✓			
ActiveSync ID	✓	✓	✓	✓	✓
User/Group administration	✓	✓	✓	✓	✓
Mobile Security Management					
KIOSK Mode	✓	✓	✓	✓	✓
Samsung KNOX	✓		✓		
Containerization	✓	✓	✓	✓	✓
Passcode/Password	✓	✓	✓	✓	✓
Mobile device reset	✓	✓	✓	✓	✓
Mobile device lock	✓	✓	✓	✓	✓

Maintaining certificates	✓	✓	✓	✓	✓
Device encryption	✓	✓	✓	✓	✓
Prohibit/Allow application (un)installation	✓	✓	✓	✓	✓
Anti-Virus support					
Malware detection					
Root/jailbreak detection	✓	✓	✓	✓	✓
Data loss prevention	✓	✓	✓	✓	✓
Mobile VPN	✓	✓	✓	✓	✓
Single-Sign On support	✓	✓	✓	✓	✓
Mobile device actions (Set VPN, WiFi, APN, proxy, Cam, Bluetooth, NFC settings)	✓	✓	✓	✓	✓
Data wipe / remote wipe	✓	✓	✓	✓	✓
Supervised mode via Apple DEP		✓			
Multifactor authentification (device/app)	✓	✓	✓	✓	✓
Mobile Application Management					
Application installation	✓	✓		✓	✓
Corporate App Store	✓	✓	✓	✓	✓
Application Blacklist/Whitelist	✓	✓		✓	✓
Vendor App Store deactivation	✓	✓	✓	✓	✓
Mandatory applications	✓	✓	✓	✓	✓
ActiveSync/Corporate Exchange settings	✓	✓	✓	✓	✓
E-Mail management	✓	✓	✓	✓	✓
Per App VPN	✓	✓	✓	✓	✓
Cost control management					

Sandboxing (Secure File Container, KNOX, fizmo)	✓	✓ ✓	✓	✓
App Wrapping	✓	✓ ✓	✓	✓
Block copy/paste	✓	✓ ✓	✓	✓
App usage monitoring	✓	✓ ✓	✓	✓
Remote desktop access	✓	✓ ✓	✓	✓
Mobile Content Management				
Data management	✓	✓ ✓	✓	✓
Secure PIM (contacts, SMS, calendar)	✓	✓ ✓	✓	✓
Document management software support (sharepoint, file server)	✓	✓ ✓	✓	✓
Data synchronization	✓	✓ ✓	✓	✓
Data push	✓	✓ ✓	✓	✓
Secure web browsing	✓	✓ ✓	✓	✓
Encrypted mail attachment	✓	✓ ✓	✓	✓
MDM Services				
Deployment options (on-premise / SaaS)	✓	✓ ✓	✓	✓
Alerts	✓	✓ ✓	✓	✓
Reporting	✓	✓ ✓	✓	✓
Real-time dashboards	✓	✓ ✓	✓	✓

Table 1: Feature matrix XenMobile Pro

Conclusion

As outlined in the feature matrix, Citrix has an extensive amount of supported functionality regarding mobile device management. The feature set in combination with the market leadership makes Citrix to a MDM vendor that has to be considered in any introduction scenario. XenMobile offers an easy maintaining mobile content management with a strict focus on business applications, secure mailing, web browsing and document sharing. Additionally, mobile application management is unique with the provided WorxApp container and WorxApp Gallery. The broad range of supported functionality for all common operating systems together with the user-friendly interaction are big advantages. However, in the small in medium sized business there are some restrictions. If organizations plan to utilize a cloud based solution data protection regulations play an important role. Citrix is located in the United States of America and does not underlie the European or Austrian data protection law. More information about Safe Harbor and data regulations were mentioned in chapter 7.3. Moreover Citrix does not offer a mobility managed service and the focus is set to the large enterprise segment. Dedicated native language support and short response times are charged extra. The graduation of prices underpins that statement. Up to 500 licences the price is about € 13.- per device and user. Additional devices per User can be ordered supplementary. The support and consultation is done by resellers and troubleshooting happens via ticketing system.

9.2.2 Airwatch

Figure 11: AirWatch
(AirWatch Inc., 2014)

AirWatch Incorporation was founded in 2003 and is located in the United States of America. Originally AirWatch served enterprise mobility management solution exclusively. In 2014 VMware acquired AirWatch and expanded their product portfolio. Due to the high experience and the long market participation, AirWatch can offer an integrated platform which consists of all areas of mobile device management. The platform itself is scalable, modular and flexible. Hence, it addresses both large and small enterprises which are looking out for lightweight and cost effective solutions. Customers can choose between cloud based and on-premise MDM solution which both offer all areas of MDM. The majority of customers are in the market sectors of airlines, pharmarcy, energy and retail.

Advantages of AirWatch

- Market leader
- Huge experience
- Broad range of MDM features
- Aggressive pricing and flexibility
- Integrated Business intelligence (BI)

Disadvantages of AirWatch

- Containerization mostly over third party vendors
- Suboptimal technical support, especially for on-premise customers
- Direct technical language support only available in the United States

(AirWatch Inc., 2014; Gartner Inc., 2013)

EMM capabilities

Feature	Android	iOS	Windows Phone 8	Blackberry OS	Symbian
Mobile Asset Management					
IMEI/IMSI status	✓	✓	✓	✓	✓
Roaming status					
Battery status	✓	✓	✓	✓	✓
GPS localization	✓	✓	✓	✓	✓
Firmware information	✓	✓	✓	✓	✓
Mobile device manufacturer	✓	✓	✓	✓	✓
Mobile device model	✓	✓	✓	✓	✓
Current language	✓	✓	✓	✓	✓
Installed software	✓	✓	✓	✓	✓
Service history	✓	✓	✓	✓	✓
Network information	✓	✓	✓	✓	✓
Enrolment date	✓	✓	✓	✓	✓
Last MDM-client connection	✓	✓	✓	✓	✓
Last inventory update	✓	✓	✓	✓	✓
Certificate validity	✓	✓	✓	✓	✓
Activation lock status	✓	✓	✓	✓	✓
Supervised status		✓			
ActiveSync ID	✓	✓	✓	✓	✓
User/Group administration	✓	✓	✓	✓	✓
Mobile Security Management					
KIOSK Mode	✓	✓	✓	✓	✓
Samsung KNOX	✓		✓		
Containerization	✓	✓	✓	✓	✓
Passcode/Password	✓	✓	✓	✓	✓
Mobile device reset	✓	✓	✓	✓	✓
Mobile device lock	✓	✓	✓	✓	✓

73

Maintaining certificates	✓	✓	✓	✓	✓
Device encryption	✓	✓	✓	✓	✓
Prohibit/Allow application (un)installation	✓	✓	✓	✓	✓
Anti-Virus support					
Malware detection					
Root/jailbreak detection	✓	✓	✓	✓	✓
Data loss prevention	✓	✓	✓	✓	✓
Mobile VPN	✓	✓	✓	✓	✓
Single-Sign On support	✓	✓	✓	✓	✓
Mobile device actions (Set VPN, WiFi, APN, proxy, Cam, Bluetooth, NFC settings)	✓	✓	✓	✓	✓
Data wipe / remote wipe	✓	✓	✓	✓	✓
Supervised mode via Apple DEP		✓			
Multifactor authentification (device/app)					
Mobile Application Management					
Application installation	✓	✓	✓	✓	✓
Corporate App Store	✓	✓	✓	✓	✓
Application Blacklist/Whitelist	✓	✓	✓	✓	✓
Vendor App Store deactivation	✓	✓	✓	✓	✓
Mandatory applications	✓	✓	✓	✓	✓
ActiveSync/Corporate Exchange settings	✓	✓	✓	✓	✓
E-Mail management	✓	✓	✓	✓	✓
Per App VPN	✓	✓	✓	✓	✓
Cost control management	✓	✓			

74

Sandboxing (Secure File Container, KNOX, fizmo)	✓	✓ ✓	✓	✓
App Wrapping	✓	✓ ✓	✓	✓
Block copy/paste	✓	✓ ✓	✓	✓
App usage monitoring	✓	✓ ✓	✓	✓
Remote desktop access	✓	✓ ✓	✓	✓
Mobile Content Management				
Data management	✓	✓ ✓	✓	✓
Secure PIM (contacts, SMS, calendar)	✓	✓ ✓	✓	✓
Document management software support (sharepoint, file server)	✓	✓ ✓	✓	✓
Data synchronization	✓	✓ ✓	✓	✓
Data push	✓	✓ ✓	✓	✓
Secure web browsing	✓	✓ ✓	✓	✓
Encrypted mail attachment	✓	✓ ✓	✓	✓
MDM Services				
Deployment options (on-premise / SaaS)	✓	✓ ✓	✓	✓
Alerts	✓	✓ ✓	✓	✓
Reporting	✓	✓ ✓	✓	✓
Real-time dashboards	✓	✓ ✓	✓	✓

Table 2: Feature matrix AirWatch ProSuite

Conclusion

AirWatch offers a broad amount of mobile device management functionality with a focus on mobile security management (MSM), personal information management (PIM) and mobile content management (MCM). The scalability, language support and the aggressive pricing compared with Citrix XenMobile are the main benefits of AirWatch. Moreover, AirWatch serves as a lightweight mobile device management system which means that the enrolment and configuration are quite easy and straight forward. Mobile application management (MAM) is supported over a huge amount of mobile devices which increases the efficiency of remote distribution, maintenance and auditing. If organizations have high demands on supported operating systems with a broad range of functionality AirWatch has to be considered. On the other hand there are some restrictions in the small and medium sized business. Data protection and Safe Harbor are topics due to the location of AirWatch and their cloud servers. Although there are data centers located in the European Union it cannot be guaranteed that the compliance with data protection law is given to one hundred percent. If multifactor authentication, anti-virus support and malware detection are important for organizations other MDM products have to be chosen. Mobility managed services and technical native language support are not offered by AirWatch directly, which makes troubleshooting quite time and cost consuming. Dedicated native language support and 24/7 support is only available in the United States. Regarding licence fees AirWatch established two approaches. Device-based licencing (cloud and on-premise) which is recommended for organizations in which employees use a single device and user-based licensing (cloud) which is recommended for organizations in which employees use multiple devices (up to 3 devices included). Additionally there is a difference regarding licence fees if organizations use a cloud based solution or an on-premise solution.

The utilization of the whole management suite results in following licence fees:

		Cloud solution	On-premise solution
Device-based month	**per**	€ 7,50	€ 8,90
User-based month	**per**	€ 14,90	n.a.

Table 3: Licence fee model - ProSuite (AirWatch Inc., 2014)

9.2.3 Mobilelron

Figure 12: Mobilelron
(Mobilelron Inc., 2015)

Mobilelron Incorporation is located in Mountain View in the United States of America. It was founded in 2007 and has an annual revenue from round about 70 million Euros. Mobilelron investigated a lot in research and development before they entered the market. Due to that fact Mobilelron served as a pioneer in the mobile device management market. The product portfolio consists of all parts of mobile device management. Enterprise mobility is the main focus and the high experience and long market participation have made Mobilelron to a market leader in enterprise mobility. The complete MDM solution offers products in the mobile application management and mobile content management which are unique. The sales process is typically for software vendors. Via channel partners and resellers the global market can be penetrated. The platform itself is scalable, modular and flexible. Three different MDM packages are offered to appeal to small as well as large enterprises and to support different areas of interest. In that context Mobilelron contributes to a lightweight and cost effective solution.

Advantages of Mobilelron

- Market leader
- Huge experience
- Complete mobile OS support
- Layered Security model
- Fast product development and release management
- Focused on mobile management totally

Disadvantages of Mobilelron

- Support via partners or resellers
- Suboptimal technical support
- Direct technical language support only available in the United States

(Mobilelron Inc., 2015; Gartner Inc., 2013)

EMM capabilities

Feature	Android	iOS	Windows Phone 8	Blackberry OS	Symbian
Mobile Asset Management					
IMEI/IMSI status	✓	✓	✓	✓	✓
Roaming status	✓	✓	✓	✓	✓
Battery status	✓	✓	✓	✓	✓
GPS localization	✓	✓	✓	✓	✓
Firmware information	✓	✓	✓	✓	✓
Mobile device manufacturer	✓	✓	✓	✓	✓
Mobile device model	✓	✓	✓	✓	✓
Current language	✓	✓	✓	✓	✓
Installed software	✓	✓	✓	✓	✓
Service history	✓	✓	✓	✓	✓
Network information	✓	✓	✓	✓	✓
Enrolment date	✓	✓	✓	✓	✓
Last MDM-client connection	✓	✓	✓	✓	✓
Last inventory update	✓	✓	✓	✓	✓
Certificate validity	✓	✓	✓	✓	✓
Activation lock status	✓	✓	✓	✓	✓
Supervised status		✓			
ActiveSync ID	✓	✓	✓	✓	✓
User/Group administration	✓	✓	✓	✓	✓
Mobile Security Management					
KIOSK Mode	✓	✓	✓	✓	✓
Samsung KNOX	✓		✓		
Containerization	✓	✓	✓	✓	✓
Passcode/Password	✓	✓	✓	✓	✓
Mobile device reset	✓	✓	✓	✓	✓
Mobile device lock	✓	✓	✓	✓	✓

Maintaining certificates	✓	✓	✓	✓	✓
Device encryption	✓	✓	✓	✓	✓
Prohibit/Allow application (un)installation	✓	✓	✓	✓	✓
Anti-Virus support	✓	✓	✓	✓	✓
Malware detection	✓	✓	✓	✓	✓
Root/jailbreak detection	✓	✓	✓	✓	✓
Data loss prevention	✓	✓	✓	✓	✓
Mobile VPN	✓	✓	✓	✓	✓
Single-Sign On support	✓	✓	✓	✓	✓
Mobile device actions (Set VPN, WiFi, APN, proxy, Cam, Bluetooth, NFC settings)	✓	✓	✓	✓	✓
Data wipe / remote wipe	✓	✓	✓	✓	✓
Supervised mode via Apple DEP		✓			
Multifactor authentification (device/app)	✓	✓	✓	✓	✓
Mobile Application Management					
Application installation	✓	✓		✓	✓
Corporate App Store	✓	✓		✓	✓
Application Blacklist/Whitelist	✓	✓	✓	✓	✓
Vendor App Store deactivation	✓	✓		✓	✓
Mandatory applications	✓	✓		✓	✓
ActiveSync/Corporate Exchange settings	✓	✓	✓	✓	✓
E-Mail management	✓	✓	✓	✓	✓
Per App VPN	✓	✓	✓	✓	✓
Cost control management	✓	✓	✓	✓	✓

Sandboxing (Secure File Container, KNOX, fizmo)	✓	✓	✓	✓	✓
App Wrapping	✓	✓	✓	✓	✓
Block copy/paste	✓	✓	✓	✓	✓
App usage monitoring	✓	✓	✓	✓	✓
Remote desktop access	✓	✓	✓	✓	✓
Mobile Content Management					
Data management					
Secure PIM (contacts, SMS, calendar)	✓	✓	✓	✓	✓
Document management software support (sharepoint, file server)	✓	✓	✓	✓	✓
Data synchronization	✓	✓	✓	✓	✓
Data push	✓	✓	✓	✓	✓
Secure web browsing	✓	✓	✓	✓	✓
Encrypted mail attachment	✓	✓	✓	✓	✓
MDM Services					
Deployment options (on-premise / SaaS)	✓	✓	✓	✓	✓
Alerts	✓	✓	✓	✓	✓
Reporting	✓	✓	✓	✓	✓
Real-time dashboards	✓	✓	✓	✓	✓

Table 4: Feature matrix MobileIron EMM Platinum

Conclusion

MobileIron is as aforementioned a pioneer in mobile device management. All areas of mobile device management are supported with a broad range of functionality. The only feature restriction occurs with windows phone application distribution and installation. All other features are supported on all considered mobile operating systems. The technology and the huge experience are the main benefits of MobileIron compared with other vendors. Like AirWatch, MobileIron offers a lightweight mobile device management system to guarantee a comfortable and easy enrolment and configuration of mobile devices. With the EMM Platinum product suite, MobileIron provides all features in the fields of mobile application management (MAM), mobile content management (MCM), mobile security management (MSM) and mobile device management (MDM) with various mobile applications (e.g. Docs@Work). Organizations with a heterogeneous infrastructure can be provided with all features of MobileIron due to the complete operating system support. That enhances business process optimization, productivity and efficiency of mobile users. Regarding data protection, MobileIron offers not only on-premise solutions. It is possible to go for a cloud based solution which is hosted by different partners around the world. However, it has to be seen critically which type of content and data is transmitted directly to MobileIron and therefore possibly in the United States. Moreover mobility managed services and technical native language support are not offered directly. Dedicated support from MobileIron is only available for large enterprises. The licence fees are charged on a device-based licence model. With less than 250 licenced devices a fixed rate is charged. With more than 250 mobile devices the licence fees are charged per device at a constant rate.

	Cloud solution	On-premise solution
Device-based per month with less than 250 devices	€ 1.4650,00	€ 2110,00
Device-based per month with more than 250 devices	€ 5,45	€ 8,44

Table 5: Licence fee model (MobileIron Inc., 2015)

This fact indicates that organizations with few mobile devices have to pay higher licence fees. On the top of the licence model is the support. Typically, standard support is included in the licence fees. Premium support can be ordered separately.

9.2.4 Samsung EMM

Samsung **Knêx**

Figure 13: Samsung Electronics
(Samsung Electronis, 2014a)

Samsung Electronics was founded in 1969 and is one of the global players regarding consumer electronics and especially mobile devices. The Samsung headquarter is loacted in Seoul (South Korea). The business areas of Samsung Electronics are widespread. From LED televisions over notebooks, camcorders to smart-phones or tablets. Since the consumeration of IT and the growing mobile market, Samsung Electronics has investigated a lot in mobile security. The multi-layered Android security concept with Trusted Boot and TrustZone-based Integrity Measurement Architecture (TIMA) are innovations from Samsung Electronics. Since 2014 Samsung Electronics has entered the mobile device management market to enhance their business fields and to support extensive mobile security for their smart-phones. Samsung EMM is the product for mobility management which consists of all parts of mobile device management. Due to their commercial presence and the fast and accurate product development Samsung has to be considered. Since 2014, Samsung EMM has grown in the fields of mobile application management, mobile asset management, mobile security management and especially in mobile content management. Many MDM vendors around the world offer Samsung KNOX Workspace – Hard- and Software secured container application – integration for their MDM solutions. The platform of Samsung EMM is very clear. The packages are offered to appeal to all kinds of customers. From private to small enterprises until large enterprises Samsung Electronics offers different solutions. The pricing policy is very aggressive to gain an accurate market share as fast as possible.

Advantages of Samsung EMM

- Market Challenger
- Huge experience
- Layered Security model
- Focused on mobile security management
- Opinion Leader

Disadvantages of Samsung EMM

- Support via partners or resellers
- Complete mobile OS support
- Suboptimal technical support
- Direct technical language support only via partners
- Restricted feature set for non-Samsung devices

(Samsung Electronics, 2014a; Gartner Inc., 2013)

EMM capabilities

Feature	Android	iOS	Windows Phone 8	Blackberry OS	Symbian
Mobile Asset Management					
IMEI/IMSI status	✓	✓			
Roaming status	✓	✓			
Battery status	✓	✓			
GPS localization	✓	✓			
Firmware information	✓	✓			
Mobile device manufacturer	✓	✓			
Mobile device model	✓	✓			
Current language	✓	✓			
Installed software	✓	✓			
Service history	✓	✓			
Network information	✓	✓			
Enrolment date	✓	✓			
Last MDM-client connection	✓	✓			

Last inventory update	✓	✓			
Certificate validity	✓	✓			
Activation lock status	✓	✓			
Supervised status		✓			
ActiveSync ID	✓	✓			
User/Group administration	✓	✓			
Mobile Security Management					
KIOSK Mode	✓	✓			
Samsung KNOX	✓				
Containerization	✓	✓			
Passcode/Password	✓	✓			
Mobile device reset	✓	✓			
Mobile device lock	✓	✓			
Maintaining certificates	✓	✓			
Device encryption	✓	✓			
Prohibit/Allow application (un)installation	✓	✓			
Anti-Virus support					
Malware detection					
Root/jailbreak detection	✓	✓			
Data loss prevention	✓	✓			
Mobile VPN	✓	✓			
Single-Sign On support	✓	✓			
Mobile device actions (Set VPN, WiFi, APN, proxy, Cam, Bluetooth, NFC settings)	✓	✓			
Data wipe / remote wipe	✓	✓			
Supervised mode via Apple DEP		✓			

Multifactor authentification (device/app)	✓	✓			
Mobile Application Management					
Application installation	✓	✓			
Corporate App Store	✓	✓			
Application Blacklist/Whitelist	✓	✓			
Vendor App Store deactivation					
Mandatory applications	✓	✓			
ActiveSync/Corporate Exchange settings	✓	✓			
E-Mail management	✓	✓			
Per App VPN	✓	✓			
Cost control management					
Sandboxing (Secure File Container, KNOX, fizmo)	✓	✓			
App Wrapping	✓	✓			
Block copy/paste	✓	✓			
App usage monitoring	✓	✓			
Remote desktop access					
Mobile Content Management					
Data management	✓	✓			
Secure PIM (contacts, SMS, calendar)	✓	✓			
Document management software support (sharepoint, file server)					
Data synchronization	✓	✓			
Data push	✓	✓			
Secure web browsing	✓	✓			

85

		✓	✓			
	Encrypted mail attachment	✓	✓			
MDM Services						
	Deployment options (on-premise / SaaS)	✓	✓			
	Alerts					
	Reporting	✓	✓			
	Real-time dashboards	✓	✓			

Table 6: Feature matrix Samsung EMM Premium

Conclusion

Samsung EMM entered the market in 2014 and focused on supporting their hardware portfolio. As the feature matrix highlights Android and iOS are supported in the meanwhile. In all areas of mobile device management Samsung EMM is competitive and offers a well-established range of functionality. However Windows Phone, Blackberry OS and Symbian are not supported, which makes it not applicable if a heterogeneous information technology infrastructure exits. Although the release plan of Samsung Electronics contains a lot of additional features for Android, iOS and Windows Phone they are not implemented yet. Examples are automatic alerts, remote desktop access, malware detection or cost control management. The strict focus is set on mobile application management and mobile security management where the system performs very well. Based on a secured container with Samsung KNOX, web applications and native mobile applications are supported completely. Single sign on, distribution over the air, application controlling and maintaining are some features why Samsung EMM has to be considered during a mobile device management introduction scenario. The system itself is again lightweight and easy to use. If Samsung KNOX capable devices are used the universal management client is installed out of the box which makes the enrolment process very comfortable. As aforementioned Samsung EMM provides features for all areas of mobile device management but the focus is on mobile security management and mobile application management. If organizations and their employees own Samsung KNOX capable devices all kinds of MDM initiatives can be implemented without losing functionality. That enhances business process optimization, productivity and efficiency of mobile users. Regarding data protection Samsung EMM offers only a cloud based solution where data is stored and transmitted in data center located continental. A big advantage is the huge partner landscape of Samsung Electronics. Mobility managed services, technical and direct language support are offered. Samsung Electronics offers dedicated support for all their customers. The licence model and the pricing are uncomplicated. Samsung KNOX Premium, which is the full MDM suite, results in € 0,80 per device and Samsung KNOX Workspace, which is the container mode, is charged with € 2,08 (only device-based licencing). The support is always included in the licence fees. Mobility managed services can be ordered separately and depends on the project size.

9.2.5   7P MDM

SEVEN PRINCIPLES

Enabling Your Business

Figure 14: 7P AG
(7P AG, 2015)

Seven Principles AG was founded in 1998 and has it's headquarter in Köln, Germany. 7P is a niche player, especially in the D-A-CH (Germany, Austria and Switzerland) region that provides different solutions in the field of information technology. It can be seen as a system integrator that employs more than seven hundred staff members. One of the most widespread business area of Seven Principles is the enterprise mobility management. Due to the enormous growing market and the position as a niche player 7P has a well-known reputation in the german speaking market. The flexibility and scalability of the MDM solution helps to react on special circumstances and business requirements. The MDM product itself consists of all areas of mobile device management. Mobile application management – together with partners like Samsung Electronics – is a focused topic of Seven Principles. 7P MDM is very modular and flexible and can therefore be introduced in many organizations, regardless of their business field. Hence, the different product packages are offered to appeal to all kinds of customers. Testimonials like ÖBB, Erste Bank Sparkasse or ProSibenSat.1 Media AG underpins that statement. Large enterprises as well as small and medium sized enterprises trust in 7P MDM.

Advantages of 7P MDM

- Complete mobile OS support
- Aggressive pricing and flexibility
- Native language support
- Mobility managed services (outsourcing of operations)
- Regular consultation

Disadvantages of 7P MDM

- Niche player
- Restricted feature set based on market requirements

(7P AG, 2015; Gartner Inc., 2013)

EMM capabilities

Feature	Android	iOS	Windows Phone 8	Blackberry OS	Symbian
Mobile Asset Management					
IMEI/IMSI status	✓	✓	✓		✓
Roaming status	✓	✓			✓
Battery status	✓	✓			✓
GPS localization	✓	✓			✓
Firmware information	✓	✓	✓		✓
Mobile device manufacturer	✓	✓	✓		✓
Mobile device model	✓	✓	✓		✓
Current language	✓	✓	✓		✓
Installed software	✓	✓			✓
Service history	✓	✓	✓		✓
Network information	✓	✓			✓
Enrolment date	✓	✓	✓		✓
Last MDM-client connection	✓	✓	✓		✓
Last inventory update	✓	✓	✓		✓
Certificate validity		✓			
Activation lock status		✓			
Supervised status		✓			
ActiveSync ID	✓	✓	✓		✓
User/Group administration	✓	✓	✓		✓
Mobile Security Management					
KIOSK Mode	✓	✓			
Samsung KNOX	✓				
Containerization	✓	✓	✓		
Passcode/Password	✓	✓	✓		✓
Mobile device reset	✓	✓	✓		✓
Mobile device lock	✓	✓			✓

Maintaining certificates	✓	✓	✓		✓
Device encryption	✓		✓		✓
Prohibit/Allow application (un)installation	✓	✓			
Anti-Virus support	✓				
Malware detection	✓				
Root/jailbreak detection	✓	✓			
Data loss prevention	✓	✓	✓		
Mobile VPN	✓	✓	✓		
Single-Sign On support	✓	✓	✓		
Mobile device actions (Set VPN, WiFi, APN, proxy, Cam, Bluetooth, NFC settings)	✓	✓	✓		
Data wipe / remote wipe	✓	✓	✓		✓
Supervised mode via Apple DEP		✓			
Multifactor authentification (device/app)					
Mobile Application Management					
Application installation	✓	✓			✓
Corporate App Store	✓	✓	✓		✓
Application Blacklist/Whitelist	✓	✓			✓
Vendor App Store deactivation	✓	✓	✓		
Mandatory applications	✓	✓			✓
ActiveSync/Corporate Exchange settings	✓	✓	✓		✓
E-Mail management	✓	✓	✓		
Per App VPN		✓			
Cost control management	✓				

90

Sandboxing (Secure File Container, KNOX, fizmo)	✓	✓	✓		✓
App Wrapping	✓	✓			
Block copy/paste	✓	✓			
App usage monitoring		✓			
Remote desktop access	✓	✓			
Mobile Content Management					
Data management	✓	✓	✓		
Secure PIM (contacts, SMS, calendar)	✓	✓			
Document management software support (sharepoint, file server)	✓	✓	✓		
Data synchronization	✓	✓	✓		
Data push	✓	✓	✓		
Secure web browsing	✓	✓			
Encrypted mail attachment		✓	✓		
MDM Services					
Deployment options (on-premise / SaaS)	✓	✓	✓		✓
Alerts	✓	✓	✓		✓
Reporting	✓	✓	✓		✓
Real-time dashboards	✓	✓	✓		✓

Table 7: Feature matrix 7P MDM

Conclusion

Seven Principles offers different features in all areas of mobile device management. They do not set the focus on functionality because mainly all MDM vendors provide a comparable feature set. Due to the fact that 7P MDM is a niche product the competitive advantages are the native language support, data protection regulations, mobility managed services and certifications in cloud computing and product security. Besides the soft facts, 7P MDM offers mobile application management (MAM), mobile asset management (MAM), mobile content management (MCM) and mobile security management (MSM) for the most common requirements as the feature matrix has pointed out. Supporting and optimizing of business processes are main objectives. Therefore remote distribution, maintenance, support and monitoring are mandatory. 7P provides a lightweight mobile device management system for the enrolment process and for MDM types (on-premise, cloud based). If organizations look for a regional MDM vendor which is a specialist in the small and medium sized market 7P MDM has to be considered. Compliance with the data protection law is given to one hundred percentage because data centers for cloud subscribers are located in Germany and Austria. Moreover the source code is certified by TÜV Austria which means that the latest security guidelines of modern software applications are adhered. However, there are some features that are not supported by 7P MDM. If Blackberry mobile devices are required or special features like multi factor authentication are necessary 7P MDM isn`t the right choice. As aforementioned mobility managed services are offered to all organizations automatically which means, that the whole mobile device management operations can be outsourced. For additional fees Seven Principles provides a 24/7 support hotline in Austria and Germany. The licence fees are split up in different packages. The total mobile device management solution is provided per device and results in € 3,99 per month. Additionally, different options can be chosen based on the organization requirements. Secure File Container can be purchased for € 0,69 per device or cost control management for € 1,29 per device. With such a modularity 7P MDM becomes competitive against the global players.

9.3 Evaluation methods

The previous chapter highlighted and evaluated enterprise mobility capabilities of different MDM vendors based on special circumstances and criteria. The following section covers mobile device management requirements in the small and medium sized market which are necessary in order to support business processes in organizations' environment. Different criteria which are demanded by the market are indicated. A conducted quantitative survey weights important criteria to emphasize the best suitable MDM solution for these requirements.

9.3.1 Identified MDM criteria

The first step to find the best suitable MDM solution in the small and medium sized market is to indicate demanded requirements. Research, expert interviews and the professional experience in the field of mobile device management has shown that following features are mandatory in order to survive in the fast growing mobile device management market.

- *Mobile Security Management*
  - ○ Remote device Lock
  - ○ Remote data Wipe
  - ○ Passcode / Password
  - ○ Jailbreak / Root detection
  - ○ Device encryption

- *Mobile Application Management*
  - ○ Application Blacklist/Whitelist
  - ○ ActiveSync/Corporate Exchange settings
  - ○ Cost control management
  - ○ Sandboxing
  - ○ Remote desktop access

- *Mobile Content Management*
  - ○ Data management
  - ○ Secure PIM
  - ○ Data push

- *MDM Services*
  - ○ Cloud deployment option
  - ○ Reporting

Both Baresch (2015) and Bukowski (2015) underpinned that demand and mentioned that MDM vendors have a strict focus on such supported features. Business became mobile in the last years and this trend will grow enormously in the future. (Alms, 2008; Sammer, et al., 2014)

9.3.2 Weighting of important criteria

The second step of the evaluation is to weight criteria according to important requirements. The criteria definition establishes the first part which delivers the base for a quantitative conducted survey. The survey was designed to analyse business requirements in the small and medium sized market and weights most important requirements. Due to the huge amount of different features, the focus of the survey lies on the aforementioned criteria in chapter 9.3.1. To reach a significant outcome the survey was distributed to 2400 (two-thousand-and-four-hundred) organizations, which employ between one and two-hundred staff members. The return rate of the survey was 1,46%. Together with the utilization of MDM systems – 48% – and the professional experience, that indicates that the awareness of mobile device management is not given at the moment. However, the results of the survey show that organizations, which take care about mobility have a clear understanding about the topic itself. According to requirements defined in chapter 9.3.1, to qualitative aspects (chapter 9.2) and to the categorized MDM features (chapter 6) the following weighting was accomplished:

Criteria	Weighting
	w
Mobile Asset Management	
Inventory data	3
Mobile Security Management	
Remote device lock	4
Remote data wipe	5
Passcode / Password	5
Jailbreak / Root detection	2
Device encryption	3
KIOSK mode	2
Anit-Virus support	5

Mobile Application Management

Application Blacklist/Whitelist	3
ActiveSync/Corporate Exchange settings	5
Cost control management	4
Sandboxing	5
Remote desktop access	1
App Wrapping	2
Mandatory applications	2
Corporate App store	1

Mobile Content Management

Data management	5
Secure PIM	4
Data push	4
VPN	5
Secure web browsing	5

MDM Services

Cloud deployment options	3
Reporting	4
Alerting	5
Real-time dashboards	3

Qualitative aspects

German language support	5
Outsourcing of operations	2
Regular consultation	1
Direct support	5
Licence fees	4

Table 8: Criteria weighting matrix

9.3.3 Comparison of different MDM systems

The weighted criteria in chapter 9.3.2 are categorized according to the categorization of MDM features, which were aforementioned in chapter 6. Special circumstances in the small and medium sized enterprise are considered in the category qualitative aspects and are key drivers for a buying decision in the SME market. Each feature of the categories is rated between one and five points based on the supported operating systems and the defined weightings – the market share of the operating systems is used as an indicator for the rated points. With this information a comparison of selected MDM systems can be drawn as follows:

	w	XenMobile p	XenMobile w*p	AirWatch p	AirWatch w*p	MobileIron p	MobileIron w*p	Samsung EMM p	Samsung EMM w*p	7P MDM p	7P MDM w*p
Mobile Asset Management											
Inventory data	3	5	15	5	15	5	15	5	15	4	12
Mobile Security Managment											
Remote device lock	4	5	20	5	20	5	20	5	20	5	20
Remote data wipe	5	5	25	5	25	5	25	5	25	5	25
Passcode / Password	5	5	25	5	25	5	25	5	25	5	25
Jailbreak / Root detection	2	5	10	5	10	5	10	5	10	5	10
Device encryption	3	5	15	5	15	5	15	5	15	3	9
KIOSK mode	2	5	10	5	10	5	10	5	10	3	6
Anit-Virus support	5		0		0	5	25		0	3	15
Mobile Application Management											
Application Blacklist/Whitelist	3	4	12	5	15	5	15	5	15	5	15
ActiveSync/Corporate	5	5	25	5	25	5	25	5	25	4	20
Cost control management	4		4	3	12	3	12		0	3	12
Sandboxing	5	5	25	5	25	5	25	5	25	5	25
Remote desktop access	1	5	5	5	5	5	5		0	2	2
App Wrapping	2	5	10	5	10	5	10	5	10	3	6
Mandatory applications	2	5	10	5	10	4	8	4	8	4	8
Corporate App store	1	5	5	5	5	4	4	4	4	5	5
Mobile Content Management											
Data management	5	5	25	5	25	5	25	5	25	3	15
Secure PIM	4	5	20	5	20	5	20	5	20	5	20
Data push	4	5	20	5	20	5	20	5	20	3	12
VPN	5	5	25	5	25	5	25	5	25	5	25
Secure Webbrowsing	5	5	25	5	25	5	25	5	25	5	25
MDM Services											
Cloud deployoment options	3	5	15	5	15		6	5	15	5	15
Reporting	4	5	20	5	20	5	20	4	16	5	20
Alerting	5	5	25	5	25	5	25	3	15	5	25
Real-time dashboards	3	5	15	5	15	5	15	4	12	5	15
Qualitative aspects											
German language support	5	3	15	3	15	2	10	5	25	5	25
Outsourcing of operations	2		0		0		0	5	10	4	8
Regular consultation	1	3	3	3	3	2	2	3	3	5	5
Direct support	5	3	15	3	15	2	10	4	20	4	20
Licence fees	4		4		4		4	5	20	3	12
Total score	107		443		454		456		458		457
Position			5		4		2		1		3

Legend
w Weighting
p grading per featuresupport
w*p weighted grading with os-support

maximum sum of each vendor 750

Table 9: MDM system comparison

The MDM system comparison illustrates that qualitative aspects are highly important. Organizations tend to buy MDM systems based on these aspects, if the feature support is given. Niche players are welcomed on the market due to the fact that the focus is set on qualitative aspects on the most important features like remote device lock, container mode, exchange settings and Anti-Virus support.

9.4 Evaluation discussion

Appendix D shows the results of the conducted survey. The return rate of the survey was 1.46%. Together with the utilization of MDM systems – 48% – and the professional experience that indicates that the awareness of mobile device management is not given at the moment. Hence, most organizations did not contribute their attitude regarding mobility. Most participants utilize smart-phones between one to five years but struggle to implement a mobility strategy although more than 60% of them rate data security as highly important. The upcoming of the smart-phone has brought a lack of security regarding sensitive business data. Figure 15 underpins the statement that smart-phones are regularly used for checking mails or manage contacts.

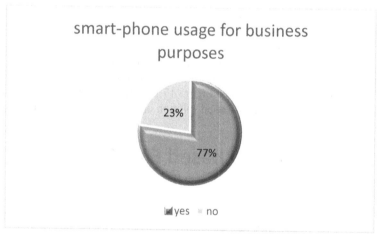

Figure 15: Smart-phone usage for business purposes

To avoid data theft most companies introduce passcode or password policies. However, they cannot guarantee the compliance without a MDM system. Hence, 48% utilize such a mobile device management system already and 60% provide their employees with needed configuration and relevant business data as Figure 16 illustrates.

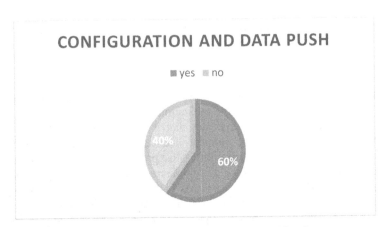

Figure 16: Configuration and data push with an EMM utilization

A key driver for the introduction of MDM system is the data protection law and the consequential private liability for chief executive officers. 71% of the participants would introduce a MDM system to avoid a private liability by enforcing data security policies like passcode protection. Under budget, and besides the data protection considerations the small and medium sized enterprise tend to utilize cloud based solutions. Figure 17 illustrates the ration between low initial costs and therefore a cloud-based solution or an on-premise solution.

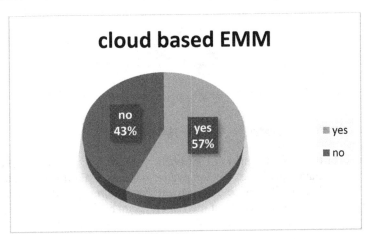

Figure 17: Attitude of MDM system types

Alerting, Reporting and deployment options are fundamental pillars for controlling, monitoring and auditing the compliance of the mobility strategy. Therefore those aspects have a huge relevance for every organization. The weighting of the importance is shown in Figure 18.

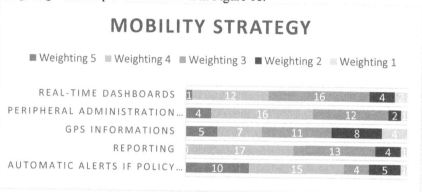

Figure 18: Important topics of the mobility strategy

Those MDM services, combined with the importance of the qualitative apsects – discussed in chapter 9.3.3 – builds a strong focus for every organization, which plans to introduce a MDM system.

Global players have a widespread feature support – illustrated in chapter 9.3.3 – but cannot provide demanded qualitative aspects in depth. In that context it depends on the requirements of the organization if a global or niche player is chosen. Different use case scenarios establish the demanded feature support for the organization. Based upon the needed features to support the mobility strategy, it is crucial that qualitative aspects fit in the vision of the organization. Increase productivity, efficiency and reduce costs at the same time are the main objectives that are pursued. A MDM system that satisfies these requirements seems to be the best fitting solution for an organization which engages a lot of effort in their mobility strategy.

10 Conclusion

Due to the consumeration of IT and the rapidly growing market of enterprise mobility the demand of systems for controlling, monitoring, maintaining and complying data protection issues is huge. Gaining more productivity, efficiency and the growth of mobile applications are drivers for enterprise mobility. Retrieving data, utilizing enterprise applications or accessing information is common today. In this context Basso and Redmann (2012) pointed out that the MDM market will rapidly grow in the future. The forecast of the market value underpins this statement. Smart-phones were originally launched as consumer products in order to support people in their daily activities. The second generation of enterprise mobility and the rapidly changing requirements in organizations introduced the smart-phone into business. Nowadays mobile devices are utilized for business purposes like checking e-mails, manage contacts and appointments. That has brought a lack of security in the existing information and technology infrastructure. Data that is distributed around the world, cannot be secured accordingly and so the compliance with data regulations is not given anymore. To achieve the desired security level, organizations search for new opportunities to maintain that issues. Especially, the small and medium sized market has special requirements which have to be addressed accordingly. That's the reason why mobile device management systems were introduced.

The master thesis takes a deeper look into several areas which are involved into this topic. Based on a definition of MDM and EMM the market size and evolution of the MDM market is summed up in the first chapters. Additionally, different mobile device types and mobile platforms are highlighted and a mobile device management categorization is established, which emphasizes supported features of MDM systems. Supporting different mobile platforms and considering features in all areas of interest is crucial for every MDM system. Chapter 6 categorizes following features:

- Mobile Asset Management (MDM)
- Mobile Application Management (MAM)
- Mobile Content Management (MCM)
- Mobile Security Management (MSM)

Due to the manifold feature set of each MDM system and the problem, that there is no defined standard for it, an evaluation is complex and expensive. Introducing a MDM system is quite difficult and has to be planned well. Defining use case scenarios and requirements are the first steps during an introduction and have to be done by any organization. Regardless the requirements, buying criteria have to be established in order to evaluate the best fitting MDM system. The MDM system evaluation in chapter 0 considers an established standard guideline feature matrix, which aims to make MDM systems comparable regarding their functionality. Prototype testing emphasizes features and integrates them into categories. The conducted survey highlights most important requirements in the small and medium sized enterprise. Based on the gathered Information and identified MDM market requirements, the particular criteria are weighted accordingly in order to evaluate chosen MDM systems. To don't burst the scope of the thesis the huge amount of existing MDM systems is qualified based on the Gartner Magic Quadrant. Gartner himself categorizes MDM systems into global players, challengers, visionaries and niche players. The choice of MDM vendors, to be evaluated, has fallen to three global players, one challenger and one niche player. That guarantees the consideration of special circumstances like licence fees or native language support. Through expert interviews, research and the professional experience the identification of demanded requirements is filtered out. A conducted survey determines most important requirements and helps to compare MDM systems based on the aforementioned categorization. By comparing and measuring the weighted criteria the MDM vendor that fits mostly is determined afterwards. The winner of the evaluation is the challenger Samsung EMM. However, during an introduction the evaluation result has to be seen critically, because every organization has its own requirements. In that context the system comparison matrix of this thesis – chapter 9.3.3 – serves as a first indicator and has to be adapted to special organization circumstances. During an introduction any organization will be confronted with decisions regarding data protection, type of MDM system, incident and problem management and different MDM initiatives. Those problem areas and identified benefits will influence organization by selecting an appropriate MDM system. Chapter 7 and chapter 8 focuses on those problem areas and benefits and highlights them in detail.

The utilization of a MDM system in organizations environment supports the security and collaboration with mobile end users. Distribution of internal developed applications, the segregation of private and business area and defining policies for the business area usage are enabler for a utilization of MDM systems. However, nowadays there has to be a business case that strengthens the awareness for mobile device management. Such a business case could be the distribution of an in-house mobile application or a business strategy to separate private from business to establish a work-life balance. In all other cases the awareness is given at the moment. The results of the survey (Appendix D) underpin this statement. Especially, in the small and medium sized market the mobile device management approach is still in the initial phase, although the market value and the demand is very high. Additionally, it has shown that the cone of uncertainty regarding MDM is too high to feel comfortable with that topic.

Bibliography

7P AG, 2015. *Seven Principles.* [Online]
Available at: http://7p-mdm.de/
[Accessed 12 2 2015].

AirWatch Inc., 2014. *AirWatch.* [Online]
Available at: http://www.air-watch.com/solutions
[Accessed 1 12 2014].

Alms, D., 2008. *Understanding Mobility Management [pdf].* [Online]
Available at:
http://get.visagemobile.com/rs/visagemobile/images/mobilitymanagementwhitep
aper.pdf
[Accessed 10 12 2014].

Asgar, A., 2013. *What is Mobile Device Management?.* [Online]
Available at: http://technicafe.net/2013/05/mobile-device-management.html
[Accessed 17 2 2015].

Baresch, M., 2015. *Enterprise Mobility Management* [Interview] (16 1 2015).

Basso, M. & Redman, P., 2012. *Critical Capabilities for Mobile Device
Management,* Stamford: Gartner.

BSI, 2013. *Bundesamt für Sicherheit in der Informationstechnik - Mobile Device
Management - Allianz für Cyber-Sicherheit [pdf].* [Online]
Available at:
https://www.google.com/url?sa=t&rct=j&q=&esrc=s&source=web&cd=1&ved=
0CB8QFjAA&url=https%3A%2F%2Fwww.allianz-fuer-
cybersicherheit.de%2FACS%2FDE%2F_downloads%2Fanwender%2Fmobilese
c%2FBSI-
CS_052.pdf%3F__blob%3DpublicationFile&ei=9yfiVLCnKIrlUtGwgogG&usg
=AFQj
[Accessed 16 2 2015].

Bukowski, A., 2015. *Enterprise Mobility Management* [Interview] (15 1 2015).

Bundeskanzleramt RIS, 2015. *Datenschutzgesetz 2000.* [Online]
Available at:
https://www.ris.bka.gv.at/GeltendeFassung.wxe?Abfrage=bundesnormen&Geset
zesnummer=10001597
[Accessed 16 2 2015].

Chloe, A., 2012. Google 'Project Glass' Replaces the Smartphone With Glasses.
PC Magazine, 1 4.

Citrix Inc., 2015. *Citrix XenMobile.* [Online]
Available at:
http://www.citrix.de/products/xenmobile/overview.html?posit=glnav
[Accessed 19 2 2015].

Citrix TechTarget, 2013. *Citrix.com [pdf].* [Online]
Available at:
http://www.citrix.com/content/dam/citrix/en_us/documents/products-
solutions/mdm-and-beyond-rethinking-mobile-security-in-a-byod-world.pdf
[Accessed 10 12 2014].

Forbes Inc., 2013. *Forbes Magazine.* [Online]
Available at: http://www.forbes.com/sites/tomkemp/2013/02/19/as-mobile-
device-management-becomes-commoditized-whats-next-for-mdm/
[Accessed 12 12 2014].

Gartner Inc., 2013. *Magic Quadrant for Mobile Device Management Software.*
[Online]
Available at: https://www.gartner.com/doc/2494216/magic-quadrant-mobile-
device-management
[Accessed 18 2 2015].

Harris, J., Ives, B. & Junglas, I., 2012. *IT Consumerization: When Gadgets Turn
Into Enterprise IT Tools [pdf].* [Online]
Available at: http://informationstrategyrsm.files.wordpress.com/2012/09/it-
consumerization-when-gadgets-turn-into-enterprise-it-tools.pdf
[Accessed 10 12 2014].

Johnson, M., 2011. *Mobile Device Management: What you Need to Know For It
Operations Management..* Brisbane: Emereo Pty Limited.

Kantar Group, 2014. *Kantar Worldpanel.* [Online]
Available at: http://www.kantarworldpanel.com/global/smartphone-os-market-share/
[Accessed 10 1 2015].

Kersten, H. & Klett, G., 2012. *Mobile Device Management.* Heidelberg: Jehle Rehm GmbH.

Klünter, O., 2014. *Mobile Betriebssysteme im Vergleich: Firmentauglichkeit, Sicherheit, MDM..* [Online]
Available at: http://www.searchnetworking.de/meinung/Mobile-Betriebssysteme-im-Vergleich-Firmentauglichkeit-Sicherheit-MDM
[Accessed 20 1 2015].

Markets and Markets, 2014. *Mobile Device Management Market by Solutions. Global Advancements, Market Forecast and Analysis (2014 - 2019).* [Online]
Available at: http://www.marketsandmarkets.com/PressReleases/mobile-device-management.asp
[Accessed 12 12 2014].

Micthell, R. L., 2014. *MDM tools: Features and functions compared..* [Online]
Available at: http://www.computerworld.com/article/2497055/mobile-device-management/mdm-tools-features-and-functions-compared.html
[Accessed 22 1 2015].

MobileIron Inc., 2015. *MobileIron.* [Online]
Available at: https://www.mobileiron.com/de/losungen
[Accessed 10 2 2015].

Open Automotive Alliance, 2015. *Open Automotive Alliance.* [Online]
Available at: http://www.openautoalliance.net/
[Accessed 14 1 2015].

Sammer, T., 2013. *The New Corporate Mobile IT: Understanding the Second Generation.* Schaan: Gutenberg.

Sammer, T., Back, A. & Walter, T., 2014. *Mobile Business. Management von mobiler IT in Unternehmen.* Zürich: buch & betz GmbH.

Samsung Electronics, 2014. *Samsung Electronics.* [Online]
Available at: http://www.samsung.com/at/home
[Accessed 1 12 2014].

Samsung Electronis, 2014a. *Samsung KNOX EMM.* [Online]
Available at: https://www.samsungknox.com/de/products/knox-emm
[Accessed 9 12 2014].

TechTarget Inc., 2013. *Why corporate device ownershipt could make a comeback.* [Online]
Available at: http://searchconsumerization.techtarget.com/feature/BYOD-vs-COPE-Why-corporate-device-ownership-could-make-a-comeback
[Accessed 18 2 2015].

TechTarget Inc., 2014. *What is a Tablet?.* [Online]
Available at: http://searchmobilecomputing.techtarget.com/definition/tablet-PC
[Accessed 9 12 2014].

TechTarget Inc., 2015a. *What is a Phablet?.* [Online]
Available at: http://whatis.techtarget.com/definition/phablet
[Accessed 10 1 2015].

TechTarget Inc., 2015b. *Smartphone.* [Online]
Available at:
http://searchmobilecomputing.techtarget.com/definition/smartphone
[Accessed 10 1 2015].

Appendix A: Expert interview Bukowski – 7P

Is it advisable for MDM vendors, under the consideration of the market conditions and the variety of Apple's application programming interfaces, to introduce mobile device management features in their products?

Definitely. Based on the closed platform approach Apple is a pioneer on the market and determine the direction. Therefore, mainly all MDM vendors implement available features as fast as possible. Additionally the provided API is well defined and programming interfaces are open for third party vendors.

Is it an advantage that the branding of the network providers has been omitted?

Of course. That fact has made update and patch management much easier. With Apple devices the branding was never a topic and therefore easier to introduce.

In the business world a global trend of segregation private from business activities can be observed. How does MDM vendors notice that fact?

I can totally agree with that statement. Therefore a huge amount of software vendors develop container solutions for mobile devices. Such solutions are offered and integrated by all MDM vendors. Safezone, Samsung KNOX or similar solutions are good products. Even Apple extended the sandboxing principle since iOS7 and is always a pioneer when containerization comes in to place.

Is Microsoft with Windows Phone 8 competitive on the mobile market?

Yes since the release of WP8 definitely. This is the reason why Seven Principles and many other MDM vendors have integrated all available features in their MDM product. Additionally, container solutions like Samsung KNOX will be available for Windows Phone in the future.

Blackberry has lost a high amount of market share in the last few years. Is this a reason why MDM vendors stop to integrate Blackberry OS features in their MDM products?

Yes. It makes no sense to support a platform which is probably no longer available in the future respectively not in the same version. The effort of implementing features is too high for a too low market share.

Why Symbian is integrated by many MDM vendors?

There are a few big customers that utilize Symbian based on their historical development. However, that fact will change in the future and even 7P will think about providing Symbian in following releases.

Which part of the EMM is the most important one and responsible for the daily business?

Mobile Security Management. Besides the proper core topics like MAM, MCM and MIM that part is responsible to define policies and measures to control, maintain und react on breaches and security lacks.

Should organizations utilize operating systems which allow data transmission between mobile applications or don't offer a container solution?

Definetely not. Since they compromise the safety and are not compliant with the latest data protection regulations.

According to the data protection law "DSG2000" chief execution officers are privately liable for any damage or disclosure of sensitive data. How does the MDM industry recognize that?

That extraction of law helps MDM vendors and provides many opportunities to strengthen the awareness of customers. Private liability can be avoided with the definition of appropriate security policies. A passcode policy could help since the mobile device is secured appropriately.

Which services are demanded by costumers, besides typical MDM features, to choose a MDM solution?
<ul><li>Managed mobility services (outsourcing of operations)</li><li>Native language support</li><li>Regular consultation</li><li>Price aggressiveness</li><li>Direct contact</li></ul>

Which features are mandatory for every MDM solution? What are the demands of the small and medium sized market?
<ul><li>Cost control management</li><li>Remote data wipe/ device lock</li><li>Jailbreak/Root detection</li><li>Mailmanagement</li><li>Data management</li><li>Data push</li><li>PIM</li><li>Passcode/Password</li><li>Roaming status</li><li>Application management/Rollout</li></ul>

Appendix B: Expert interview Baresch – Samsung

Must sensitive corporate data be controlled on all mobile devices?

Personal Information Management is highly important on every mobile device. Even on smart watches if they are running independently in the future. Sensitive data can't stay on devices without any control mechanism. That's the reason why they have to be managed.

Can that statement be applied for future technologies like glasses or cars?

Surely. The new generation of glasses or cars offer PIM (Personal Information Management) functionality out of the box.

In the business world a global trend of segregation private from business activities can be observed. How does MDM vendors notice that fact?

I can totally agree with that statement. Samsung focuses on the KNOX platform which is a solution that provide a secure hard- and software container. The product is nearly integrated by every MDM vendor around the world.

Is the control mechanism for conventional notebooks over a mobile device management system accepted by the market? (Especially in the SME market)

Currently not. Therefore most MDM vendors does not provide such feature. In the small and medium sized market such control mechanism is adopted poorly.

Blackberry has lost a high amount of market share in the last few years. Is this a reason why MDM vendors stop to integrate Blackberry OS features in their MDM products?

Definitely. Samsung focuses on their products and support them to one hundred percentage. Only if in-house devices are supported appropriately Samsung will integrate other platforms. The integration of other platforms depends on the market share and the strategic alliance with partners. Blackberry lose market share due to their unstable situation. The effort is too high to concentrate on platforms with low market share.

Why Symbian is integrated by many MDM vendors?

Symbian was a pioneer in mobile operating systems and especially in the Scandinavian region there are a few big customers. However, the integration of Symbian will not be supported in following releases.

Which part of the EMM is the most important one and responsible for the daily business?

Mobile Application Management. Segregate private from business areas are highly important and therefore the whole application management can be split up in those two areas.

Should organizations utilize operating systems which allow data transmission between mobile applications or don't offer a container solution?

Such operating systems will disappear from the market if they could not react on such requirements. The industry seeks for such solutions.

Which services are demanded by costumers, besides typical MDM features, to choose a MDM solution?
<ul><li>Direct contact</li><li>Outsourcing of operations (especially in the SME market)</li><li>Aggressive price structure</li></ul>

Which features are mandatory for every MDM solution? What are the demands of the small and medium sized market?
<ul><li>Container solutions (segregate private from business areas)</li><li>Remote data wipe</li><li>Device lock</li><li>Jailbreak/Root detection</li><li>Mailmanagement</li><li>Data management</li><li>Data push</li><li>Application management</li></ul>

Appendix C: Quantitative Survey

The following survey is conducted within the scope of a market evaluation for enterprise mobility management systems.

It is directed to chief executive managers and information technology decision makers in small and medium sized enterprises in Austria (1 to 200 employees). The survey aims to analyse the current market situation for enterprise mobility and to record important requirements of an enterprise mobility management (EMM) system.

The purpose of the survey is to collect important requirements, underpin data protection regulations and strengthen the awareness of all involved parties of mobility strategy in organizations. In addition essential features of EMM systems are emphasized to ensure a proper market evaluation of various EMM system vendors.

Answer the questions as honest and complete as possible. Answering all questions should not take longer than fifteen minutes.

1. How many employees does your organization have?

   ☐ 1-10
   ☐ 10-50
   ☐ 50-100
   ☐ 100-200
   ☐ over 200

2. Since how many years does your organization utilize smart-phones or tablets?

   ☐ Less than 1 year
   ☐ Between 1 and 5 years
   ☐ More than 5 years

3. How important is data security of sensitive business data for you? (E-Mail, photos, documents)

☐ Very important
☐ important
☐ not important
☐ I think about it
☐ Doesn`t matter

4. Do you regulary use your mobile device (smart-phone, tablet,...) to check your mails and manage contacts?

☐ yes
☐ no

If yes, how do you secure your mobile device against data theft or in case of   loss?
(Multiple choices possible)
☐ remote device lock
☐ remote data wipe
☐ Passcode or Password
☐ Device encryption
☐ Not at all

5. Do you use an enterprise mobility management system (EMM) to maintain your mobile devices?

☐ yes
☐ no
☐ I think about it
☐ What is that?

6. Would you utilize an EMM system to provide your employess with needed configuration and relevant business data at any time?

☐ yes
☐ no

7. According to the data protection law in Austria "DSG" §14 each chief executive officer is liable for data theft of sensitive data privately. Would you as a chief executive officer introduce an EMM system to avoid this liability?

☐ yes
☐ no

8. How important are **inventory** data of your mobile devices for you? (installed software, roaming status, GPS location, device manufacturer, device model, and so on)

☐ Very important
☐ important
☐ not important
☐ I think about it
☐ Doesn't matter

9. You already utilize an EMM system or think about an introduction in your organization. Which features regarding **mobile application management** are most important?
(Assign points between 1 to 5, with 5 being the highest priority)
__ Application blacklists / whitelists
__ Automatic mail management
__ Cost control management of all mobile devices
__ Strict segregation between private and business data (Container App)
__ Corporate App Store
__ Mandatory applications for all employees
__ App Wrapping
__ other: _____

10. The content of many mobile applications supports business processes directly. Thus, sales material can be transferred to mobile devices to provide necessary data to sales representatives to ensure fast and accurate availability. How important is/would **content management** for you? (Assign points between 1 to 5, with 5 being the highest priority)

    __ Central file management for all employees
    __ Personal information secure storage (contacts, calendar, SMS)
    __ Encrypted connections between mobile devices and the business (VPN)
    __ Connection to the existing network infrastructure (file server)
    __ Encrpyted mail attachements
    __ Secure web browsing
    __other: _____

11. Security is in many organizations highly important in the local information technology structure. Which **security aspects** do/would you use for mobile devices in your organization?
(Assign points between 1 to 5, with 5 being the highest priority)

    __ Only in-house applicatoins are allowed.(KIOSK Modus)
    __ Anti-Virus support
    __ Certificate management of mobile devices
    __ Remote device lock
    __ PinCode request to unlock mobile devices
    __ Remote data wipe
    __ Device encryption
    __ Business area has to be isolated (Container)
    __ Multifactor authentication (e.g.: username/password and SMS confirmation)
    __ other: _____

12. If you want to utilize an EMM system which apsects are crucial for a buying decision?
(Multiple choices possible)

- ☐ German language support (phone or mail)
- ☐ Direct contact
- ☐ Low licence fees and initial costs
- ☐ Regular consultation
- ☐ Outsourcing of operations
- ☐ Supporting multiple MDM initiatives
  (Organization buys the device or employees utilizes his private owned device)

13. Do you want to keep the initial costs low? Would you accept a cloud based EMM solution?

- ☐ yes
- ☐ no

14. Is the easiness of handling an EMM system important for you? This means that your employees are equipped with identical mobile devices!

- ☐ Very important
- ☐ Important
- ☐ Not important
- ☐ Doesn`t matter
- ☐ All mobile devices have to be supported

15. How important are following topics in your mobility strategy?
(Assign points between 1 to 5, with 5 being the highest priority)
___ Automatic alerts if policy breaches occurs
___ Reporting
___ GPS information's
___ Peripheral administration (WiFi, NFC, Bluetooth, Camera)
___ Real-time dashboards
___ other: _____

16. Do you prefer a regional EMM vendor instead of a global player if your requirements could be fulfilled?

☐ Yes
☐ No
☐ Yes, if the price fits.

Appendix D: Survey analysis

1. How many employees does your organization have?

Employees	Count
1-10	18
10-50	13
50-100	1
100-200	2
over 200	1

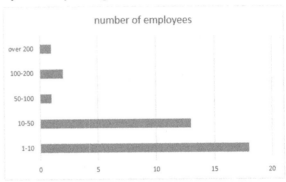

2. Since how many years does your organization utilize smart-phones or tablets?

less than 1 year	3
between 1 and 5 years	20
more than 5 years	12

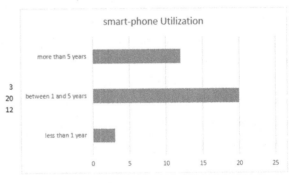

3. How important is data security of sensitive business data for you? (E-Mail, photos, documents)

very important	21
important	10
not important	3
I think about it	0
doesn't matter	1

4. Do you regulary use your mobile device (smart-phone, tablet,…) to check your mails and manage contacts?

yes	27
no	8

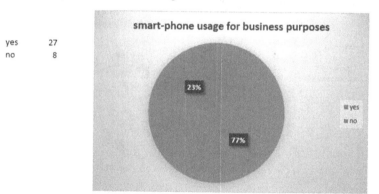

If yes, how do you secure your mobile device against data theft or in case of loss? (Multiple choices possible)

remote device lock	6
remote data wipe	3
passcode or password	18
device encryption	5
not at all	4

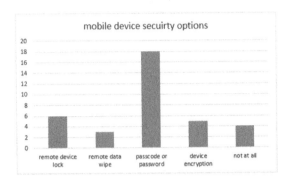

5. Do you use an enterprise mobility management system (EMM) to maintain your mobile devices?

yes	3
no	17
I think about	5
What is that	10

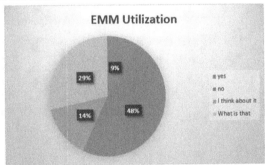

6. Would you utilize an EMM system to provide your employees with needed configuration and relevant business data at any time?

yes   21
no   14

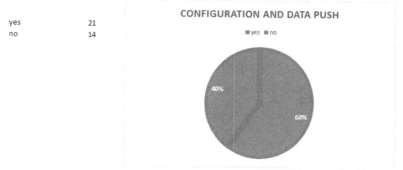

7. According to the data protection law in Austria "DSG" §14 each chief executive officer is liable for data theft of sensitive data privately. Would you as a chief executive officer introduce an EMM system to avoid this liability?

yes   25
no   10

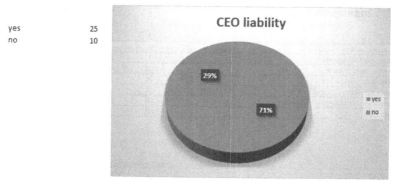

8. How important are **inventory** data of your mobile devices for you? (installed software, roaming status, GPS location, device manufacturer, device model, and so on)

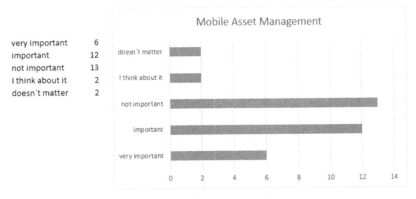

very important	6
important	12
not important	13
I think about it	2
doesn't matter	2

9. You already utilize an EMM system or think about an introduction in your organization. Which features regarding **mobile application management** are most important?

	5	4	3	2	1	Weighting factor
Application blacklists / whitelists	5	5	18	1	6	3
Automatic mail management	13	12	3	1	6	5
cost control management	11	13	7	1	3	4
Container App	11	8	9	2	5	5
Corporate App Store	2	6	7	8	12	1
Mandatory applications for employees	2	5	11	7	10	2
App Wrapping	0	5	13	7	10	2

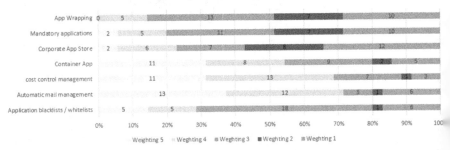

10. The content of many mobile applications supports business processes directly. Thus, sales material can be transferred to mobile devices to provide necessary data to sales representatives to ensure fast and accurate availability. How important is/would **content management** for you?

	5	4	3	2	1	Weighting factor
Central file management for all employees	14	10	5	3	3	5
Personal information secure storage	12	14	4	2	3	4
Encrypted connections (VPN)	16	9	6	2	2	5
Connection to file server	11	11	7	3	3	4
Ecrypted mail attachements	15	9	4	5	2	5
Secure web browsing	17	11	3	0	4	5

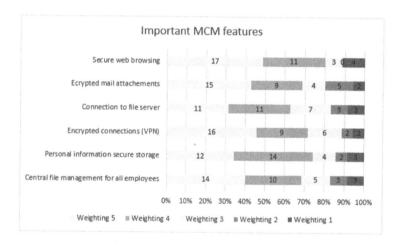

11. Security is in many organizations highly important in the local information technology structure. Which **security aspects** do/would you use for mobile devices in your organization?

	5	4	3	2	1	Weighting factor
KIOSK Modus	3	7	8	9	8	2
Anti-Virus support	16	8	8	2	1	5
Certificate management	5	8	12	5	5	3
Remote device lock	6	12	13	3	1	4
PinCode request to unlock	16	14	4	0	1	5
Remote data wipe	14	6	10	4	1	5
Device enryption	9	13	10	2	1	4
Container mode	11	9	8	4	3	5
Multifactor authentification	9	5	12	4	5	3

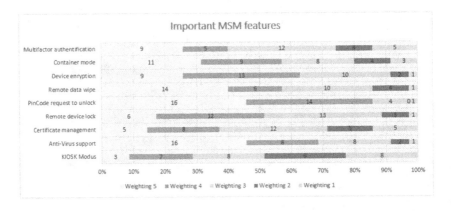

12. If you want to utilize an EMM system which apsects are crucial for a buying decision?

		Weighting factor
German language support (phone or mail)	28	5
Direct contact	28	5
Low licence fees and initial costs	26	4
Regular consultation	10	1
Outsourcing of operations	14	2
Supporting mulitple MDM initiatives	10	1

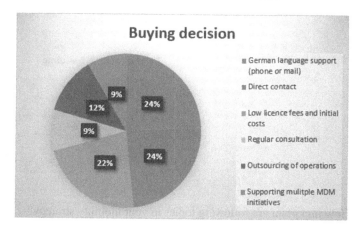

13. Do you want to keep the initial costs low? Would you accept a cloud based EMM solution?

yes	20
no	15

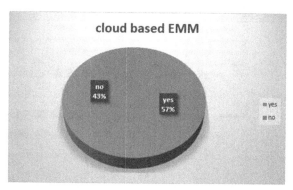

14. Is the easiness of handling an EMM system important for you? This means that your employees are equipped with identical mobile devices!

very important	4
important	18
not important	7
doesn't matter	3
All mobile devices have to be supported	3

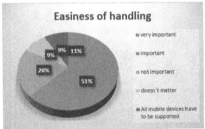

15. How important are following topics in your mobility strategy?

	5	4	3	2	1	Weighting factor
Automatic alerts if policy breaches occurs	10	15	4	5	1	4
Reporting	0	17	13	4	1	4
GPS informations	5	7	11	8	4	3
Peripheral administration (Wi-Fi, NFC,...)	4	16	12	2	1	4
Real-time dashboards	1	12	16	4	2	3

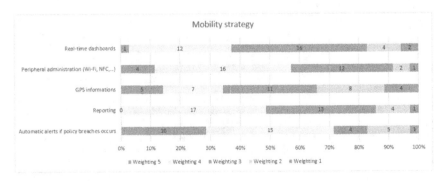

16. Do you prefer a regional EMM vendor instead of a global player if your requirements could be fulfilled?

yes	21
no	2
Yes, if the price fits	12

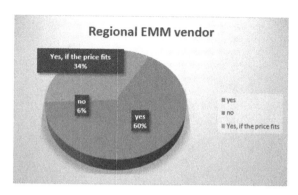

Printed in the United States
By Bookmasters